FREE YOURSELF FROM FEAR

D0827329

By the same author:
Hypnosex
Self-hypnosis

Valerie Austin

FREE YOURSELF FROM FEAR

Self-hypnosis for anxiety,
panic attacks and phobias

Thorsons
An Imprint of HarperCollinsPublishers

Thorsons

An Imprint of HarperCollins*Publishers*

77–85 Fulham Palace Road,

Hammersmith, London W6 8JB

Published by Thorsons 1998

10 9 8 7 6 5 4 3 2

A catalogue record for this book

is available from the British Library

ISBN 0 7225 3553 8

Printed and bound in Great Britain by

Caledonian International Book Manufacturing Ltd, Glasgow

To Gil Boyne
who retrieved my lost memory
in true Hollywood style.
Thanks a mil, Gil!

CONTENTS

ACKNOWLEDGEMENTS

In my previous books I have listed many people who have helped me in my work, and I still accept that they have been instrumental in my research in the past. But for this book I would like to thank my clients, especially the ones who have become friends.

University of Sabah Malaysia, and University of Psychology (UKM), Kuala Lumpur.

Dato Abdul Halim Othman for his invitations to speak at the Universities, and his far-seeing recognition of a need for hypnotherapy research. The New Straits Times for their support.

Dato Dr Halim Abdul Wahab for an excellent conference facility at the Promenade Hotel, Sabah. Philip and executive staff at the Flamingo Hotel in Kuala Lumpur for the wonderful attention on my courses.

Sabre Said for his kind attention and for publishing my book 'Stop Smoking in One Hour' (Berita Publishing).

And to my special friends Johnny, Shukri and the delightful Sity for the setting up of the Austin Hypnotherapy Institute at Langkawi.

Roy – you always write your own!

Pierre Marcar for his friendship and some very elegant suggestions included in the book. Philip for some nifty designs.

Mary Lines, Mandy and Richard, Mourine Brockwell, Rudy Danials, John Zuli, and Jim Kerr for his new vision.

FOREWORD

I first became aware of Valerie Austin when she came for treatment of a two year memory loss after being injured in an auto crash.

In a dramatic 90 minute hypnotherapy session Valerie's amnesia was cured and her memory was restored.

Her amazing cure convinced her to become a hypnotherapist so that she could help others. After extensive training Valerie was awarded her Diploma and Certification and began her practice in the UK.

Since then she has written several books and developed programmes for stopping smoking, weight loss and sexual enhancement, all of which have been valuable contributions to the field of self-help.

Her latest work, *Free Yourself From Fear,* is a new and radical approach to effective relief from fear and phobias. I strongly recommend *Free Yourself From Fear* to all victims of irrational and phobic fears and believe it will become 'required reading' for mental health counselors.

Gil Boyne, Executive Director of the American Council of Hypnotherapist Examiners.

PREFACE

When I was asked to address the University of Malaysia Sabah, School of Psychology and Social Work, and to conduct a workshop for 150 teachers, students and people in the working environment, I needed to present hypnosis in a way that could be understood by every member of the varied audience. Having been deeply uncomfortable with many of the traditional labels used in hypnotherapy (such as regression, past life, etc.) – and feeling that they would sound less daunting under another title as they seem to be so far removed from the world as we know it (dare I say old-fashioned, even?) – I knew I had to find a better way to convey what hypnosis is all about.

Freud, Jung and all the early masters of hypnosis would turn in their graves if they could see how rigidly their techniques are followed, without regard for the present-day high technology that has opened new avenues into the mind. So for the purposes of the workshop I enlisted the help of a colleague of mine, a film director with a scientific education, a sound knowledge of computers and familiarity with hypnosis (having videoed and studied my courses several years ago). Together we began to explore the similarities between the mind and the computer. I had just finished doing some research on cloning for my last book and I suddenly felt that in a way humanity had already 'cloned' the brain, in a sense, without realizing it. Computers and the information that has been produced on using them come directly from the workings of our own minds, as if our brains were gradually training us in how to use them, constantly upgrading the techniques and allowing us to keep inventing more sophisticated procedures – a bit like the way in which you teach a child to read. In the beginning you introduce reading by showing a child picture books. You then move on to illustrated books with very simple words, and then gradually work up to more complicated reading matter.

For the many people who use computers, here is an aid to mapping computer terms to the mind. (If you are not computer-friendly, don't worry: you don't have to use this to understand the message of this book).

A USEFUL GUIDE TO FRONT-LOADING YOUR MIND BEFORE WE BEGIN

Computer (hardware) =	Brain
Software (disc) =	Knowledge
File/Folder =	Memories store
Current software =	Belief structure/Current self
Searcher/File retriever =	Regression
Remote viewing =	Past, present and future exploration of the mind
Overload/Computer crash =	Trauma/Nervous Breakdown
E-mail =	Mind telepathy
Repairing =	Healing
Windows '95/Bill Gates, etc. =	Gestalt/Freud/Jung
Technician =	Hypnotherapist/NLP/psychologist/psychiatrist
Engineer =	Consultant
Hacker =	Specialist in hypnosis

The knowledge I gained from new technology and working with computers gave me the shift I needed to update my own understanding and teaching of hypnosis. The results were positive and exciting, and I am at the moment working closely with three universities in Malaysia to bring the discipline of hypnotherapy into its own. This is a joint venture with my Institute in Langkawi, Malaysia, which is founded specifically to fund research into the true success rate of hypnotherapy.

WHAT IS HYPNOTHERAPY?

Hypnotherapy is a collection of techniques used when in a trance. Its strategies are geared for the subconscious, not for the conscious. The conscious analysing is left for the psychologist. To use psychology with hypnosis is rather like trying to combine dentistry with chiropody. They are two distinct disciplines, although a person may sometimes find that he or she needs both.

There are many very reputable and distinguished hypnotherapists, but still the treatment is regarded with great scepticism. I will try to change some of this, and in so doing give you a more accurate description of what is happening to you when you suffer from phobias, panic attacks or anxiety that are creating chaos in your life.

One

HYPNOTHERAPY FOR FEAR

PANIC ATTACKS, ANXIETIES AND PHOBIAS

Anxiety can create panic attacks, and panic attacks can be linked to an unspecified phobia. Panic attacks, phobias and anxiety go hand in hand and are on the increase in the suave, polished, refined, civilized 1990s: Fear of cars, driving, sex, motorways, bridges, tubes, planes, spiders, snakes and many, many more. The solution is hidden in the inner mind and not readily available to the conscious mind. Being put in a tight vest as a baby can manifest into a fear of lifts later in life; a forgotten contract you privately made to yourself when a loved one has had a serious, life-threatening accident – 'I will always be tidy if he/she lives' – can develop into a compulsion for tidiness or constant washing of hands.

I had a fear of driving after a severe car accident, with the usual hot sweats and terrors; a fear of dragonflies and dentists also became part of my life. These lasted for years before I realized they could be overcome.

THE ROAD TO FEAR

The case histories in this book will give you an insight into how fascinating and complicated the mind can be. Modern hypnotherapists have, as you will see, much in common with computer hackers. They find the source of a problem and remove it. The better the hacker, the more cleared you are of 'mind debris'. We are now able to use some of the new mind-technology and adapt it for self-help.

For the purposes of this discussion I will use the term 'fear attacks' to encompass phobias, panic attacks and anxiety issues. The fear which is behind these conditions is worsened by the increase in materialism, and the stress this creates, in our society. Yet such fear can just as easily be erased by hypnosis, using the power of the mind to adjust your lifestyle.

For sufferers, the road to fear is treacherous, made worse because they feel they have no control. The results are loss of confidence and self-worth and increasing frustration, feeding energy into these unwanted emotions and making them strong and significant. You become a victim of your own emotions; negative emotions gone wild, unleashed in disarray, like rebellious, disruptive children. Your life becomes continuously affected and you have to cater more and more for your affliction. The fear is like a caged, ferocious animal which is let out too often without discretion, causing chaos.

There has been so much written about this distressing sequence of events, but very little actual help has been offered. There are many similarities in the causes and effects of anxiety, phobias and panic attacks, so that although you may suffer from, for example, a phobia, you may find that the chapter on anxiety has some useful exercises for you. There are many variables when it comes to why we suffer from fears, but one thing that can be relied on is that hypnosis has the highest success rate by far. It is quick and to the point, and can help you to find a release from your fear.

There are two ways hypnosis can be used:

1 self-hypnosis
2 with the help of a qualified hypnotherapist

The discussion of self-hypnosis in this book is thorough and includes examples and positive exercises. If you should decide that you need the help of a hypnotherapist, the recommendations in Chapter 8 can help to point you in the right direction.

Let's take a look at the advantages and drawbacks of self-hypnosis versus a hypnotherapist.

The non-trauma-related fear attack – that is, one that does *not* stem from an early or very deep-seated emotional shock – can be fixed easily and permanently in a very short space of time through self-help methods. If you suffer from a trauma-related problem, however, then it is likely that more advanced methods in hypnosis are necessary, requiring the guidance of a well-trained hypnotherapist. The therapist's success rate depends on the methods used and level of training he or she has received. Some modern specialists can take as few as two or as many as five sessions to achieve a successful result, while others get a result more or less immediately (in minutes rather than hours), but produce a lower success rate over the long term, as results are not always permanent. It's a numbers game and, as long as you understand the reasons behind the successes and failures, then you won't be one of those people who have heard of someone who was treated with hypnosis but found it didn't work, therefore mistakenly believing that hypnosis would not be of any help for you either. Hypnosis has a very high success rate – in the region of 90 per cent for phobias with one specific technique, and around 50 per cent for another. I can assure you this is very high compared with other therapies, which are usually no more than 27 per cent successful.

With suggestion hypnosis and self-help techniques, as featured in this book, the success rate ranges from 30 to 60 per cent. If the reader were not to put the necessary commitment into using the methods, then obviously this would drag the success rate down. But I am going to presume that you are the type of person who realizes that following the instructions and taking them seriously will give you a chance of overcoming your fear.

Drawbacks that Affect Change

Let's look at the reasons that would prevent the process working for a person being treated by a hypnotherapist. The therapist may be excellent in dealing with other problems – for example, depression – and yet not have good techniques for overcoming fear attacks. Or the sufferer may have a hidden motive for holding on to the problem: for example, it stops them from having to work. They may on the other hand be burdened with an old but active programme in their mind that ensures that they do not succeed. This would mean that the person would probably have to be treated for the underlying source of the problem before the fear can be released.

Fortunately, these are the exceptions to the rule. Phobias are generally easier to treat for the hypnotherapist, as against the anxiety and panic attack, because the source of a phobia is generally easier to locate. But, of course, it depends on the type of underlying trauma and the amount of digging needed to find how the problem started in the first place.

Advantages of Self-help

Where does this leave the person who would like to treat the fear attack themselves, rather than see a hypnotherapist? The advantages are that self-help is inexpensive and takes only a little effort to achieve a very healthy success rate. Even if the fear attack is not cleared up completely, the information that you will have learned about how and why the mind works in the way it does will be a great advantage both for yourself and for a hypnotherapist should you choose to use one at some time in the future. At best you will solve the problem entirely yourself; at worst it will help you to find a therapist who can help you.

STRESS AND ANXIETY

Stress is an inextricable part of panic attacks, anxiety and/or phobias. Understanding one could prevent the others.

When you get a Wall Street broker using the responses a cave man used to fight the elements, you've got a problem.

BOSTON UNIVERSITY PSYCHIATRIST PETER KNAPP

The 'fight or flight' response was identified by Dr Walter Cannon in the 1930s. Stress is the reaction of the autonomic nervous system in defending itself against attack, real or imagined. It is an instinctive reaction when we are in danger, a primitive survival response that all humans and animals respond to. The nervous system releases adrenalin to assist in the 'fight or flight' response. Once the threat subsides, the system returns to normal because the adrenalin has been used up either in fighting or fleeing the danger. If the adrenalin remains unused, however, and remains in the system, the result is what we know of as stress.

So What Happens When You Are Stressed?

When under stress, your heart rate increases to ensure that there is enough blood pumped through the necessary tissues to transport oxygen and nutrients to the cells. When the heart rate increases, blood pressure rises and breathing quickens and becomes more shallow. Adrenaline and other important hormones are released into the bloodstream, and the liver gets rid of stored sugar, to cope with the excess of energy your body is calling for.

The digestive system is affected, with less blood flow, and so the appetite subsides, while the blood flow to the brain and other major muscles increases. Blood leaves the hands and feet, making them feel cold – this protects against the possibility of heavy blood loss should these extremities suffer injury. All senses are heightened and the pupils in the eyes dilate; the body begins to perspire in order to cool itself.

All this happens in a flash without you actually being aware of it when you are in danger. But when you are not in any genuine physical danger, just over-anxious or stressed out, then you'll notice the discomfort these changes cause.

It is useful to note that since diseases are caused by a variety of different factors, we cannot blame stress alone. But there is a strong link between stress and the onset of disease. Stress can contribute to the effects of:

❖ cardiovascular disorders: high blood pressure, irregular heart rate, hypoglycaemia, stroke
❖ neuro-muscular disorders: back pain, chronic pain, bruxism (tension in the jaw), clumsiness, neck and shoulder pain, muscle cramps, migraine, muscle spasm
❖ respiratory and allergic disorders: asthma, allergies, breathing dysfunctions, infectious diseases
❖ circulatory problems: cold hands and feet
❖ immunological disorders: cancer
❖ gastro-intestinal disturbances: diarrhoea, constipation, metabolic dysfunction
❖ skeletal problems: arthritis
❖ skin disorders: perspiration
❖ dental problems
❖ substance abuse: alcoholism, drug abuse, overeating
❖ emotional disturbance: depression, emotional instability, dwelling on the past or future
❖ mental dysfunction: forgetfulness, fatigue, insomnia, learning difficulties
❖ sexual dysfunction

and, of course, anxiety, fears and phobias.

Headaches and migraine, as mentioned, are a direct response to stress, as are shingles. In fact, shingles are a very good example of the power of the mind. It is proved that shingles are directly related to worry and stress.

THE THREE TYPES OF STRESS

1 Physical stress, which is created by environmental factors such as extremes in temperature, environmental pollution, constant noise or electric shock. Researchers also include factors such as injury, surgery, hypoglycaemia, prolonged exercise or an inadequate supply of oxygen as factors contributing to physical stress.

2 Psychological stress, which is affected by the way we feel, our attitudes and the way we react to circumstances that are threatening, either real or imagined.

3 Psychosocial stress, which involves arguments or conflicts with family members, neighbours, employers, friends or other people. On the other hand, psychosocial stress can also occur when someone has been isolated because they have not been socializing and have become insulated.

Theorists have studied and correlated stressful changes in the social environment with illness and dysfunction. Smale (1968) found that serious illness often follows separation of some kind. While Hinkle (1973) reported these views:

… that the relation of people to their society and to the people around them can influence the incidence, the prevalence, the course and the mortality of diseases seems clear enough. The questions at issue are the questions of when they do so, under what circumstances, by what mechanisms and to what extent.

American researchers have found that hassles from mundane jobs have a greater impact on health than do major life changes; that, in fact, major life changes may predominate health only because they create more mundane jobs. A survey of 210 Florida police officers conducted by psychologists Charles Spielberger and Kenneth Grier of the University of South Florida found that the officers found it much more stressful dealing with the day-to-day resistance created by what they saw as the ineffective judicial system and a hostile press than with their responsibilities for responding to and fighting crime.

Everyone reacts differently to stress. 'Stress is like a ride on a roller coaster. There are those at the front of the car, hands over head, clapping, who can't wait to go on again, and those at the back cringing, wondering how they got into this and how soon it's going to be over,' says Paul J. Rosch, President of the American Institute of Stress. Differences in perception can cause some stress to be good stress – there is even a name for it, *eustress* – or bad stress, distress. Eustress promotes productivity and facilitates our efforts, while distress leads to loss of productivity and causes health problems. One is exhilarating, the other leads to a feeling of being out of control and helpless.

Homes and Rahe, in their now famous research, developed a list of stress-related life events. Add up the points assigned to the events that apply to you: if the number reaches 150, then you are in a position that can cause enough stress for your body to react negatively.

Death of a spouse/partner	100
Divorce	73
Marital separation/End of a relationship	65
Gaol term	63
Death of close family member	63
Personal injury, illness	53
Undergoing an abortion or miscarriage	53
Getting married	50
Being made redundant	47
Marital or relationship reconciliation	45
Retirement	45
Change in family member's health (whether better *or* worse)	44
Pregnancy	40
Sexual problems	39
Addition of new family member	39
Business readjustment	39
Change in job or profession	36
Change in number of marital arguments (up *or* down)	35
Mortgage or loan over £10,000	31
Foreclosure of mortgage or loan	30
Change in work responsibilities (fewer *or* more)	29
Child leaving home	29

If the points add up to 150 at any one time, then it is a fair assumption that your mind may do something about it to relieve the pressure, especially if you refuse to relax. Those who are under stress but refuse to 'submit' – perhaps saying: 'I haven't time to be ill' – will create for themselves the scenario in which their body develops some form of disability that will force them to slow down. The body's 'survival programme' makes sure that you do survive. It will turn to radical measures to prevent you from suffering a heart attack or other major stress-related illness. You may find yourself with a nervous breakdown and be forced to stop your life as it is now or, like me, suffer a memory loss and have no choice but to slow down. But whatever your subconscious chooses, it doesn't switch back to normal once you are rested. It's as if your subconscious arranges your body for a breakdown and then gets on with monitoring your body, letting you figure your way out, perhaps to stop you in the future from abusing yourself yet again under immediate killer stress. But whatever is happening in your life, whether a build-up of stress or sliding towards the nervous breakdown, it can be halted by stress-reduction techniques and in some cases save your life.

I had a client who said she wanted to alter her sleeping pattern. She explained that her life was very successful and said she wanted to have more time in the early morning but liked to socialize into the small hours fairly regularly – a case of burning the candle at both ends. She was inquiring if she could use self-hypnosis to help take short catnaps in the day to compensate for the lost sleep at night. She had tried on her own, but admitted in her own words that she seemed to 'sabotage' every attempt. Could it be that her mind was rebelling and, if so, why? She was generally an enthusiastic and positive person and enjoyed her life very much, so what was going on?

I put her in hypnosis and gave her a post-hypnotic suggestion that when she came out of hypnosis her arms would be a lever for her stress. If she was carrying stress on board, then her arms would feel heavy, not uncomfortably, just heavy enough to indicate the level of her stress. She responded to hypnosis easily. She had said she worked on herself with meditation and it showed with her easy, deep relaxation. When she came out of hypnosis I asked her how her arms felt. 'Very heavy, even my chest feels tight,' she responded.

So, even though her life seemed to her to be going perfectly smoothly, she was carrying a lot of stress on board. I suggested we explore the reason behind this build-up in the next few sessions, during which we could also look at arranging a sleep pattern to match her lifestyle.

A colleague made a remark to me that was a rather clever way of explaining this woman's dilemma. He described it as rather like a swan gliding easily through the water. We see only elegant, graceful movement, but under the water the swan's legs are paddling like mad.

The trouble with stress is that you don't know you have it until it is at a dangerous level.

As you see in the list above, fun and excitement also create levels of stress which, when added to other, more serious problems such as marriage break-up or moving house, can be part and parcel of severe anxiety or even a breakdown. If you try to ignore or neglect the stress in your life, you will pay in years to come. Research has shown that people who have had an unhappy and dysfunctional childhood carry a special chemical which creates a condition that prompts heart attack at as young as 40 years old. Post-mortems done on people who have had to struggle constantly against hardship in order to survive suffered from scars on their heart that led to premature death.

A Little Theory

Stress theory conceptualizes that the attempt to balance or restore equilibrium is primary for the survival of the organism. Selye's stress theory (1974) holds that it is just as stressful to experience pleasure or enjoyment as to experience displeasure, since the organism's inner balance is disturbed. Both positive and negative experiences can be stressors. It has been likened to a bank balance. Every tension relieved is a debit from the chequebook of resources. Rest or change of situation is used as a credit to balance the debits, otherwise eventually the individual is overdrawn and suffers physical symptoms.

Personality factors can affect how people experience and handle stress, whether it is experienced as overwhelming and threatening or as challenge and opportunity. People need challenge. Without challenge, growth and development might never take place. There is also a paradox: some illnesses are cured by stress. As a symposium on stress had concluded, not all stress is bad for the organism.

There are, alas, those who become addicted to adrenalin. The athlete and the soldier live in the realms of constant adrenalin turn-on and can end up searching for more and more thrills and challenges in order to feel that rush.

How Stress Affects the Individual Personality

Dr Ray Roseman and his colleague Meyer Friedman conducted a famous investigation into which type of person was most likely to have a coronary. Their typical candidate for a heart attack, known as 'Type A', exhibits a habitual sense of urgency and an excessively competitive drive.

What type of personality are you? The way we handle a given situation is influenced by our disposition – our frame of mind, or temperament. When under a lot of pressure you may remain calm or become extremely tense; it is your disposition that will determine your stress level. Once you can identify your own disposition (perhaps from among the five personality types listed below) you can begin to understand, and change, the way you react to different kinds of stress.

THE FIVE PERSONALITY TYPES

1 Ambitious and Driven – this type of person (the classic 'Type A') has a strong desire for success or achievement. He or she is highly committed to career goals, extremely energetic and rarely finds time to relax. He or she is impatient, aggressive and argumentative, often feeling a strong need to dominate. Type A people set themselves high standards and cannot bear failure. They burden themselves with impossible deadlines and workloads, adding more and more stress to their lives and never pausing for breath. Although their preferred stress level is high, so is their vulnerability to the negative effects of stress.

2 Calm and Collected – this type is tranquil, even placid, and does not become easily disturbed, excited or agitated. People with this natural temperament take time to reflect and think over their achievements, and do not set themselves impossible objectives. Their

self-esteem is strong and they do not need to be domineering. They are seldom irritated by others and both give and receive affection and praise easily. Their stress level is medium to low and their vulnerability to the effects of stress is low.

3   Conscientious and Controlled – those with this type of temperament are meticulous, taking extreme care over everything required of them. They are reliable, single-minded and can often be stubborn. They can become over-obsessive in their desire to do things thoroughly. They run the risk of losing sight of long-term objectives in their pursuit of the small details. They prefer a set routine and can be thrown off-balance by the unexpected. They do not cope with change as well as the ambitious or calm type. They do not seek challenges in life. Because of their insecurity about losing control, they can suffer a lot with inner tension. Their stress level (and vulnerability to stress) is low to moderate but can be increased to very high levels at times of change.

4   Shy and Unassertive – people with this type of personality have great difficulty standing up for their rights. They are mainly concerned with pleasing others, usually in an effort to avoid conflict. They shy away from situations rather than face them. They cannot express their own needs. They often feel resentful that others take advantage of them; this creates a lot of inner tension. Their stress level is above average and their vulnerability to the effects of stress is moderate.

5   Anxious and Tense – those with this type of temperament find it hard ever to relax. They spend

most of their time worrying about what might happen rather than concentrate on what is actually going on, a habit which is not usually constructive. They are prone to panic; this becomes evident when things do go wrong. They are far too concerned with other people's judgements and evaluations, therefore their self-esteem and confidence are low. They are insecure and uncertain about changing environments and will react defensively rather than rise to the challenge of change. Their stress level and vulnerability to stress are high.

As you will have gathered, most people are in fact a combination of two or more of these generalized personality types, and no one is free from stress. But everyone can learn to handle it properly.

Stress and Lifestyle

Think of your body as a car. Your heart is the engine, your backbone the axle and suspension, your muscles are the transmission and your arms and legs are the wheels. The big difference is that the body has a built-in driver which we call the brain and nervous system. So what happens when the driver starts making mistakes?

Although I don't want to alarm you, if you are pushing yourself too much and creating stress and possibly bringing on anxiety, then you could end up triggering a malfunction of the brain. Anything that upsets the delicate environment in which the brain functions can cause tumour, infection and damage to the brain.

We rarely have to worry about our survival, as our primitive ancestors had to do every day of their lives. But we have worries that can be perceived as a threat to our lives: bills, the struggle to hold down a job and cope with personal and professional responsibilities can provoke enough worry to trigger a build-up of emotions that leads inevitably to stress overload. Once we've reached this point, even the smallest of incidents can cause a panic attack.

If you drink too much or work or worry in excess, you may be setting yourself up for a very unpleasant experience, apart from the fact it may even kill you prematurely. Hopefully, this may get you to thinking about changing your life and giving that wonderful body and mind of yours a little respect. Remember, if your body was a vintage Rolls Royce you would hardly run it to the ground or put inferior petrol in it!

IS IT TIME FOR A CHANGE?

I cannot 'stress' too much how important it is to look after yourself. Stress destroys the body's resistance to cancer, infections, illness and even the strength to overcome surgery. It weakens the immune system, making it difficult to fight off even a simple cold.

A good test to see if you have your life in order is to ask yourself if you would like to live to the ripe old age of 150. If you hold up your hands in horror at the prospect, then you should look at *why*. Could it be that you have got your life wrong and are just marking time to get through it, instead of really living it? Eliminate the thoughts of blame either for yourself or anyone else. If you look closely you will find there were plenty of decisions you could have made to improve your situation, but the good news is that there are always options, it's never too late whatever you have experienced in the past. Past experience is a good learning curve, and hard knocks and traumas, however disastrous at the time, in the future can be constructive in building your strength. But you do need to examine them to find out what you are required to learn from the situations, otherwise you may just end up repeating the same old programme over and over again.

Could it be that you've got your life wrong and are living to get through it, instead of enjoying the challenge? If it is the former then you are probably carrying around with you a small amount of stress that is constant, and added to the everyday external stresses this certainly can make a significant impact.

Since obscene amounts of money are being spent by every major drug company on research for the sole purpose of increasing our life span, in the very near future we may be looking at a pleasant, or depressing, surprise on life expectancy – whether pleasant or depressing depends on you.

The good news is that it's never too late to learn from past experience, rather than just replaying the same old program over and over again.

Whatever is happening in your life, the build-up of stress can be halted by stress-reduction techniques. For some odd reason, we in the West seem to eliminate all thoughts that we are responsible for our own stressful lives. Rationalizing that it is fate, we let ourselves take the consequences when a little work on ourselves is all that is needed. A few minutes a day can create a far better existence and enjoyment in the later years of life, instead of letting our bodies undergo wear and tear unnecessarily, growing old before our time with aches and pains that could have been prevented. What we do now affects us in 20 years' time. But at any time we can start to care for ourselves and reverse the process. Before it is too late we can use exercise the mind to relax the body, enabling direct healing.

So take a good look at your life, and although humans don't like change it may be time to take stock and consider some adjustments. I did just that a couple of years ago and dropped a few friends. I had made excuses and allowances for them for far too long. The friends I have kept are real, I feel more confident and my worries have lessened considerably. I know that if things change and I find I have made a mistake, then I will have to acknowledge it and learn.

Reducing stress, however, does not mean a completely stress-less life. It's all about how you handle it. If you aren't able to deal with it without it taking a toll on yourself and/or your family, then it is time to take stock. There will be plenty of signs if there are adjustments to make – sometimes so obvious they are almost in three-metre high neon lights.

If you are overweight, drink too much, have a short fuse and constantly catch colds or flu, what does that tell you? You don't have to walk out of your life to make it better, but start to look at yourself. Put yourself into a relaxed state and ask questions of your inner mind. It can be that simple: you have all the answers in that magnificent brain of yours. That's all I do in my profession – ask the inner mind to direct me to the problem so I can re-programme from within.

How Important Is Relaxation?

Relaxation is the answer to eternal youth. The problem is that we believe we rarely have time to relax, and if by chance we do have this spare time we would rather use it for enjoying ourselves – simple relaxation doesn't seem to be in this category, it's more like a chore, unexciting and boring. I have added a script in Chapter 6 that hopefully will encourage you to make a simple relaxing technique part of your daily routine.

If you use this technique, what are the perks? Soothing and calming your personality so it sparkles instead of grates. You think nothing of cleaning your hands, face and teeth every day; relaxation is an excellent way of clearing the debris from your mind – a preventative for constantly moaning to your friends about your lot.

It only takes a few minutes of deep breathing and emptying your mind or listening to a relaxation tape (which you can prepare from the script in this book – *see page 74*) to gain precious benefits.

A regular relaxing massage is the ultimate in body pampering, will keep you young and stimulate your blood cells, keeping body and mind in top form. Play one of your favourite relaxation tapes while you are having a massage. It surprises me how many people would rather spend their excess money on an expensive, potentially dangerous meal with rich sauces and plenty of booze instead of some serious pampering. Massage is a safe and very satisfying luxury.

Deep Breathing

Most people's breathing is very shallow; when told to take a deep breath they take a deep 'shallow' breath from the chest. Breathing exercises are the simplest and oldest way of controlling tension. First you need to practise breathing from your diaphragm. Try the following simple deep breathing exercise, in a quiet place at least three times a day, for one week. You'll be amazed at how much more calm you feel.

Place your hand on your diaphragm (just above your stomach) to check you are breathing correctly: your hand should go up and down as you breathe. Take a deep and slow breath from your diaphragm and close your eyes. Exhale fully and completely, visualizing all your troubles and anxieties gathering into a round ball, as you breathe easily and rhythmically. The ball gets bigger as you collect more of your doubts and fears and negative emotions. When you feel you have collected all the excess negative emotions, breathe in fully. Now, as you exhale slowly, imagine you are sending this ball off into space, never to return, far, far away into the galaxy. You know that ball of unwanted disruptive thoughts will safely disperse in space never to return, leaving you free and clear with positive thoughts and energy to replace all that built-up mental and emotional debris.

A Novel Relaxation Technique

It's so simple you would think everyone would be doing it: When you are anxious and feel like having a drink to calm down, why not combine your relaxation and deep breathing exercises while having a long hot bath? Give yourself half an hour, no longer, and have the temperature at about 39°C/103°F. Muscles are relaxed, circulation increases and your blood pressure is lowered. Take a deep breath and exhale fully and completely. The water movement is hypnotic to the mind; you can just close your eyes and scan your body for places that you think may be holding stress. Allow your mind to empty of all thoughts of the day. Concentrate on your body, how it feels as the water touches your arms and legs. Feel your arms and legs wanting to float and allow your breathing to become regular and slow. Enjoy the luxury of the water and the comfort of your muscles as you relax even more.

Eating Healthily

You can be sure that you are what you eat – so what does that make you if you eat a lot of junk food?

Give yourself (and your loved ones) a break: don't stuff yourselves with fatty and sugary foods, then bury your head in the sand and say those feeble little words, 'Why me?' when health problems crop up. Don't forget you can also be an accessory to a crime by not preventing it in the first place. You could be saving the life of a loved one.

Eat the basics. If you're not a vegan, fish is the food of the brain. Try to get lots of different vegetables and a selection of fruit per day, with potatoes or pasta for carbohydrate energy. Bear in mind that it's sources you need to worry about: if you can afford it, go for organic. Always choose fresh or frozen veg over the tinned kind.

Read labels carefully. There are many food ingredients and additives that can make emotional stress and anxiety that much worse:

❖ People talk about having a bar of chocolate or biscuits as an energy boost because of the sugar, forgetting that empty calories may give you an initial rush of energy, but you come down twice as fast. Slimming products that use artificial sweeteners may be doing you more damage than the weight.

❖ MSG (monosodium glutamate) is used in many foods as a 'flavour enhancer'. Those sensitive to MSG suffer symptoms including pressure on the head, seizures, chest pains, headache, nausea, burning sensations and tightness of the face. Many baby-food producers have stopped adding MSG to their products.

❖ When you're having your diet cola, note that its ingredients can cause Alzheimer's disease, osteoporosis, memory loss, asthma, eczema, loss of calcium from bone and calcification (hardening) of soft tissues. Bone mineral content and density can decrease, making it more likely that you develop osteoporosis, neurological and behavioural reactions, headaches, seizures and blindness, muscle spasms or heart trouble. People who suffer from asthma, rhinitis or urticaria may find that diet soft drinks make their symptoms worse.

❖ Calcium sulphite is used mainly as a preservative in many foods, from burgers and biscuits to frozen mushrooms and horseradish pulp. Sulphites are banned from many foods in the US, including meat, because they make old produce look fresh. They can produce side-effects of bronchial problems, flushing, low blood pressure, tingling and, in extreme cases, anaphylactic shock.

❖ Benzoic (E210) is a preservative in many low-sugar products, cereals and meat products. It inhibits the function of digestive enzymes and may deplete glycine levels, affecting hayfever, hives and asthma sufferers.

❖ Cyclamic acid and its Na and Ca salts (E952). Used as a sweetener in 'diet-energy-reduced' and 'no-added-sugar' products. Causes some skin conditions.

❖ Disodium diphosphate SAPP (E450). Used in dough-nuts, biscuits, baking powder, cheese, tinned potatoes, fish. Excessive use can cause imbalance of mineral levels, which can cause damage to bone density (perhaps contributing to osteoporosis).

❖ The beer drinker may want to note the following secret side-effects: fertility and/or memory problems. The carbon dioxide used for the 'fizz' in beer and other drinks, even water, retards ripening in vegetables and fruit and inactivates moulds and bacteria. Experimental evidence shows carbon reduces fertility significantly. Such drinks may also contain aluminium, which is used to clear water. This has been linked with Alzheimer's and osteoporosis.

❖ Flavourings can include any number of combinations of Es and additives with unknown effects.

❖ Tartrazine (E102) can cause hyperactivity in children and other allergic reactions, such as asthma.

❖　Brilliant Black BN (E151) is used in drinks, sauces, snacks, wines, cheese, etc. It should be avoided by sufferers of allergic conditions, asthma, rhinitis or urticaria.

Exercise

Take a tip from my *Slim While You Sleep* book (Blake Publishing), which suggests useful gentle exercises, or visit a gym and get some professional help to start you off. Tell the instructor what you want to achieve and he or she will give you a safe and easy programme to work at yourself.

Note

Nobody said it was going to be easy to modify your life for health. But think of the achievement and pride you will feel with a healthy body and mind. You'll be much more able to cope, without any harm to that all-important immune system.

Knowing that what is happening in your life can create illness allows you the option to work on yourself with simple relaxation techniques in order to avoid tragedy in the future. It also should be noted that the influence of the mind – our thoughts and imagination – can be more powerful than medications.

New drugs can change the chemical balance in our bodies to help correct our behaviour, leading to more problems than they solve. 'Mind' work – which, in essence, uses the mind to correct itself – does not interfere with the overall balance of chemicals that are necessary to allow us to be in natural control of our lives and feelings and, in turn, keep us stable.

Hypnosis is a perfect example of this 'mind' work. Meditation, yoga, tai chi, zen chiasu and chi gung are among the many other examples of self-healing. The difference with hypnosis is that it achieves change quickly and easily, and has by far the highest success rate when used to combat fear attacks. So let us look at the reasons why, and then how, this natural healing system works. We should, for a change, give the respect to our mind – our human computer – that it deserves and have a peek at the sophisticated software that is available to every one of us.

Two

PHOBIAS

H ypnosis is like switching the mind computer on – the therapy consists of techniques used to change the mind.

Janet Leigh has a serious phobia – she can't ever have a shower. She will never take one and makes sure she always has access to a bath on film sets or on location. If she is ever in a situation where she has no option but to take a shower, she will not use the shower curtain and always faces the door while she washes quickly. This phobia is the result of appearing in the film Psycho, in which her character met a violent death in the shower at the hands of the character played by Anthony Perkins. This horrific murder scene was so graphic, and accompanied by such memorable music and sound effects that it has stayed with her all these years. I'm sure Janet isn't the only victim of shower phobia caused by this film!

We all have fears, but they are not necessarily strong enough to cause us problems. We may not like spiders or snakes and may go out of our way to avoid them, but this is quite different from having a phobia about something. The phobic suffers the most acute fright. It is as powerful as being in fear of losing one's life. It brings on sweats, palpations of the heart, nausea, fainting and the feeling that the hairs on the arms or the back of the neck are standing on end.

A phobia is a fear and may even be exaggerated by fear of the fear itself. It is a learned response, you are not born with it. It doesn't necessarily have to have been caused by a terrible trauma; it can derive from something that now seems insignificant but made an impression on you when you were a child. Or it can be as simple as a mistaken reaction that has become a habit, or a reaction 'caught' from your parents or someone you admired – or even from someone you don't like. Phobias can be of anything imaginable, or even unimaginable. The more common fears have many interesting and complicated names, as you can see from the list at the end of this chapter. But to have a name for every known phobia would require a new dictionary. To complicate things further, a person may have a phobia about one thing when the true underlying fear is related to something quite different. Thus a therapist, doctor, psychologist or the sufferer him- or herself is left working completely blind, leading to the wrong conclusions and the result that the sufferer is still stuck with the phobia.

DESENSITIZATION AND HYPNOTHERAPY

Desensitization behaviour therapy, where a situation is created in which the sufferer is slowly and by stages brought into contact with what causes the fear, is a popular therapy but can be very traumatic. When used hand in hand with hypnosis, however, it becomes an efficient and reliable form of treatment.

If you have a fear of snakes, to desensitize yourself you would have to put yourself in a cage with a lot of snakes so that eventually you would get used to them – or that is the theory. But most people would find this a fate worse than death and prefer to put up with the problem.

The less outrageous methods of desensitizing are to coax a person gently; for example, you would get someone with a fear of spiders to look at drawings or pictures of spiders, then perhaps to look at the real thing (behind glass or in a cage), and eventually to come face-to-face with live examples. This method is slow and yet does have value, but is not suitable for everyone and holds only a moderate success rate.

Work in hypnosis offers the gentle way out. One colleague of mine uses suggestion hypnosis and then proves that it works by coaxing the phobic with a fear of spiders to hold a tarantula. He does this at the London Zoo in groups and has an excellent success rate.

PRESUMPTION IS THE CAUSE
OF MAJOR BLUNDERS!

A client of a colleague of mine – I will call her Sally – was afraid of cats. She was in her mid-twenties and had lived with this fear for as long as she could remember. The fear had heightened her instincts to the point where they were so acute that she could tell if there were a cat within a few metres, even if she couldn't see it. She would break out into blotches all over her arms and face, her heart would pound and she would go into a mild state of shock.

She was desperate to overcome this phobia because she had become engaged to a man whose mother kept several cats.

My colleague used regression – a simple technique that requests the mind to bring forward a memory from the past, usually forgotten by the conscious self, which holds vital information needed to change attitude, resulting in a change in behaviour. Once the behaviour changes, the phobia is cleared. This type of therapy ensures a permanent change, whereas the 10-minute 'quick fix' methods or mind-trick therapies, although they may sometimes be very successful, have a lower success rate.

When Sally was regressed, she went back to a time when she was asleep in her pram. A crack of thunder shocked her awake and also frightened a cat. As she opened her eyes, she saw the cat jumping over the pram. The thunder was still rolling and so she fused the frightening sound that caused her heart to race with the vision of the cat. So, the next time she saw a cat it triggered off the frightening physical feelings again. Now she was not only frightened of seeing a cat, but frightened of the fear that she experienced each time she saw a cat. The fear built up out of all proportion, ending up with her breaking out in blotches all over and experiencing the shock she could not consciously control.

Another client, Carol, came to see me about her fear of lifts and closed spaces. I regressed Carol to the first time she experienced the fear. She, too, was in a pram and her mother had put her in a liberty bodice, an old-fashioned type of thick vest. It was too tight and she was struggling to breathe. She instinctively tried to pull herself up out of the pram to get some air, but felt trapped and frightened – she panicked. This remembered breathing restriction had been triggered again when she was in enclosed spaces such as a lift, which caused her to react as she had done when she was in her pram. Panic caused her to try to escape. She would go into sheer panic when the lift doors closed. The memory of her experience in the pram was forgotten and lost to her conscious mind, while all the time it was tucked away safely in the subconscious 'memory banks'. The subconscious creates the physical response, the conscious not even knowing where it is coming from, unable to use logic to change the programme.

I had a client who wanted to train as a hypnotherapist and took one of my courses. I have to clear phobias during my course or I would lose the belief structure of the class, so I do not have the luxury of a mediocre success rate. It has to be 100 per cent. If a student wants me to demonstrate on them how I can clear phobias, I have no option but to succeed.

This student, whom I will call Susan, had a fear of spiders. The fear was so extreme that she could not touch a long-handled sweeping brush if it had been in contact with a spider, and she would go into hysterics if she saw one, however small. Her husband was so used to it he would just steer her out of the room if he saw a spider about. The fact that she could not touch a brush if it had been in contact with even a tiny spider was unusual. When I regressed her she was six years old and in a garden shed. She had been locked in the shed by the headmistress of her kindergarten school. She went through the experience graphically. She was watching the big spiders whilst hating the headmistress. Her hate was extreme and she had associated the spiders with such hate that when she saw a spider again she got angry and yelled. Thus her phobia turned on an emotion that she had presumed was fear but, in fact, was potent anger. When made aware of this in hypnosis she couldn't believe it was that simple. As this particular course was being held in a large country house, with no shortage of spiders, it wasn't long before I spotted one and called Susan. I pointed to the spider and asked if it bothered her. She smiled and shrugged her shoulders. I doubt if a quick mind-trick therapy or even suggestion hypnosis would have fixed the phobia in this case, as it stemmed from a complicated trauma structure. The exercise showed Susan that her fear was not of spiders but of the anger she had felt. The spider had just acted as a trigger, bringing back all the anger, helplessness and feeling of being out of control.

When I was doing some work on speed reading, I had a case that may help you to understand the misunderstanding that can develop round the presumed and actual source of a fear problem. In speed reading it is important for the person to use a pointer – either a pen or some other object – to point with to guide the eyes at the required speed across the page. It is difficult to do this without hypnosis. It actually involves forming a new habit, and any habit needs practice. Hypnosis enables you to form a good habit or break a bad habit (like stopping smoking). A suggestion is formed to instruct the inner mind to follow the pointer at the maximum speed for retention and concentration and the client can then speed read successfully within minutes, no practice necessary. It is so successful I will guarantee someone who takes my course at least to double their reading speed immediately, and many can treble it without any practice. Hypnosis eliminates the need for practice; that is why you can learn to stop smoking in one hour.

The gentleman, whom I will call John, found that he was feeling very uneasy doing speed reading when travelling on a tube train. He said he felt embarrassed using a pointer. He came to see me for a 'back-up' session. The back-up is a sort of fine-tuning of the mind. It required some regression therapy – going back in your mind to the past to see where the behaviour started. John had told me that he had no memories before he was six years old. In hypnosis, he was regressed to the age of four, when he pictured himself pointing at an old recluse. The recluse was a threatening figure and very bad-tempered, so John was frightened of him. John had retained this fear in his finger. So although he had presumed that his uncomfortable feeling when using the pointer stemmed from embarrassment, in hypnosis he realized that the finger had held another emotion – fear. In regression the fear was remembered; after this hypnosis session John went on to double comfortably his reading speed.

'INHERITED' AND
TRAUMA-RELATED PHOBIAS

It is possible that a trauma-related phobia can be cleared with suggestion therapy. I can only say that using regression therapy on people who have already tried suggestion therapy without success will normally uncover a trauma.

Hypnosis enables you to form a good habit or break a bad habit (like stopping smoking). A suggestion is formed to instruct your inner mind. Hypnosis eliminates the need for practice; that is why you can learn to stop smoking in one hour.

New evidence suggests we are not always in control of our minds. We need to find out how and why our fear is being fuelled and channelled with energy. Then we can starve the fear of its source, which in turn will stop the phobic attacks for ever. If the fear has been 'inherited' rather than based on some personal trauma we have experienced, then simple suggestion therapy will clear it up completely and, generally, permanently. Unfortunately, there is no way of identifying whether a phobia is trauma-based until a certain amount of treatment has been done. The information lies in the subconscious, and the only route to the subconscious is via hypnosis.

The distinction between the two sources of a phobia came to light when I treated two sisters, both with a common fear of flying. I saw Trudy for the first time six months before her sister, Alex, came to see me. I hypnotized Trudy and regressed her to the time the phobia was established. In so doing I uncovered an experience she had forgotten consciously: At the age of about five years old she was taken in a private plane by a friend of her father's. While they were in the air the

pilot tipped the plane so that she could see a swimming pool
below. The pilot was used to the plane's surging movements
created by the sudden turn, but Trudy wasn't. She felt her
stomach sink. This frightened her, anchoring a response. The
next time she boarded a plane, years later, her stomach
responded similarly. This created a fear of the fear and a
strong reaction to flying. Each time she flew, the feelings were
compounded until she had reached the point where she
couldn't even go to the airport.

When Trudy was cured of her phobia, her sister Alex
came to see me. She was going on honeymoon and needed to
control her fear. Alex decided to have her phobia treated after
seeing the positive results Trudy had achieved. When regressed
in hypnosis, I found that Alex had flown without fear as a child
and at some point she became jealous of the attention her sister was receiving because of her phobia. In response to a silent
request, Alex's subconscious granted her wish for attention by
creating a real phobia, imitating her sister's phobia without her
consciously being aware of this internal programme. Alex's
phobia was overcome easily with suggestion hypnosis (the
type demonstrated in this book), whereas Trudy's needed
more advanced therapy from a specialist.

Chapter 6 offers specific suggestions for overcoming
phobias, allowing you to choose the most suitable for your
individual condition.

Research

Some people believe that phobias are linked to a more primitive level of functioning, that we develop phobias to things that at one time in humanity's primal history would have been a threat to our survival.

Research carried out in the US surveyed a random sample of 1,000 people about their fears and phobias. Topping the resulting list were fear of illness and injury, storms, animals, the outdoors (agoraphobia), death, crowds and heights.

SOME COMMON AND NOT-SO-COMMON PHOBIAS

Acrophobia	Heights
Acuphobia	Sharp objects
Agoraphobia	Being outdoors
Ailurophobia	Cats
Alektorophobia	Chickens
Ancraophobia	Wind
Anthophobia	Plants
Anthropophobia	Human beings
Apiphobia	Bees
Arachnaphobia	Spiders
Astraphobia	Lightning
Bacteriophobia	Bacteria
Blennophobia	Slime
Brontophobia	Thunder
Chrometophobia	Money
Claustrophobia	Fear of enclosed spaces
Coprophobia	Faeces
Cynophobia	Dogs
Dendrophobia	Trees
Dermatiophobia	Skin
Dipsophobia	Drinking
Eisoptrophobia	Mirrors
Emetophobia	Vomiting
Erotophobia	Making love
Gametophobia	Marriage
Genuphobia	Knees
Graphophobia	Writing
Gymnophobia	Nudity

Haematophobia	Blood
Heliophobia	Sun
Helminthophobia	Worms
Ichthyophobia	Fish
Kakorrhapiahobia	Failure
Limnophobia	Lakes
Lyssophobia	Insanity
Monophobia	Being alone
Musicophobia	Music
Mysophobia	Dirt
Nephophobia	Clouds
Nosophobia	Disease
Odontophobia	Teeth
Ombrophobia	Rain
Ommetaphobia	Eyes
Ophidiophobia	Snakes
Ornithophobia	Birds
Pantophobia	Everything
Pediculophobia	Lice
Peniaphobia	Poverty
Psychophobia	Mind
Spheksophobia	Wasps
Taphophobia	Being buried alive
Tocophobia	Childbirth
Triskaidekaphobia	Number 13
Vaccinophobia	Inoculations
Xenophobia	Foreigners
Zoophobia	Animals

Three

ANXIETY

Breathing is usually a natural function and under the conscious control, but when fear, anger or other negative emotions creep in, then breathing can go to pot.

❖ ❖ ❖

Anxiety can cause great suffering and lead people to limit their lives in order to avoid the feared experience. It can alter their behaviour, seemingly against their will. It is damaging to the family of the sufferer: children can pick up on this emotion and may grow up feeling anxious themselves, more or less copying their role model, their parent.

Anxiety stops us from having joy in our lives. The energy used keeping this emotion going is enormous. Constant stress leaves the body vulnerable to illness and depression.

Changing the pattern of anxiety takes time and practice. You need to re-learn (or learn for the first time in your life) to meet the challenges of life with less tension, both mentally and physically.

I treated a person who thought he was fine but when hypnotized we realized how wrong he was. He was in denial and although his body was giving him the danger signs, he refused to listen. His back was as stiff as a board. His masseur had warned him but he hadn't taken it on board. Without working on creating a better strategy for life, he would certainly have been a candidate for a heart attack.

WHERE DOES ANXIETY COME FROM?

A highly emotional experience may be sufficient to set the cycle in motion. Early 'negative programming' may be at the root of the problem, although in some cases the trigger may occur later in life. There have been many documented cases where patients in surgery have been so traumatized by their experience that a phobia or long-lasting anxiety results.

Hypnosis is able to produce relaxation and lower anxiety. Its efficacy as a treatment has been proven by many clinical reports. People live with these discomforts, limit their lives and never realize that treatment is possible. Trance work, which is in effect hypnosis, can bridge the gap between thought and action and bring about positive change.

A study of 50 anxiety patients conducted by Dr Kenneth Hambley in his book *Banish Anxiety* (Thorsons) reported on the symptoms of anxiety and the percentage of people who experienced them. He states: 'No one suffered from all the symptoms at one time,' but he points out: 'Sometimes one symptom can replace another. The phenomenon is called symptom transfer.' He mentions further that almost all of the symptoms are produced by having too much adrenaline in the bloodstream, as occurs when we are under stress.

Muscle tension	67.3%
Panic attacks	56.4%
Headache	49.1%
Excessive fatigue	47.3%
Tearfulness	43.6%
Palpitations	40.0%
Dizziness	38.2%
Tremor	29.1%
Pain	23.6%
Stomach discomfort	23.6%
Breathing difficulty	18.2%
Swallowing difficulty	14.5%
Diarrhoea	9.1%

Dr Hambley explains that the anxiety sufferer fears most the severe and possibly disabling systems of the anxiety itself, even more than what causes the anxiety in the first place. This fear of anxiety symptoms is entirely understandable and logical.

Case Histories

Joseph was a 50-year-old man who decided to have a facelift. The problem was that his wife Paula was not happy with his decision. She liked his 'sagging jowls', as he called them, and his decision made her feel inadequate. She felt embarrassed when friends mentioned how much younger *he* looked, but had no intention of having surgery herself. The marriage failed. Paula complained that Joseph had changed since the operation, that he had become more aggressive and vain.

Joseph's Side of the Story

> When I looked in the mirror I was horrified by what I saw. My face was baggy and when I moved I could feel the skin under my chin jiggle about and wobble. My mates called me 'plastic face' and I looked like I had the jowls of a turkey. I would drive round with a hand over my chin so nobody noticed the fat.

He was delighted with the results.

Paula's Story

> Without doubt the operation did take 10 years off. But as a result I felt more middle-aged. I'd always considered myself to be quite young at heart, but Joseph's sudden youthful appearance made me feel frumpy and old. I also realized that I preferred his old face. Women like men with faces with a bit of character, men like Mick Jagger or Jimmy Nail. By taking away his flabby chin and his jowls, I felt as though the surgeon was removing a part of my husband that I loved. I told him that I preferred him the way the way he was, but he just said: 'Tough, it's too late.'
>
> It was so humiliating. I also felt that Joseph wanted a younger woman and that having a facelift was his way

of attracting one. He seemed to take on a new personality
after the surgery. I had always assumed we would grow
old gracefully together – how wrong could I have been?

In this case, both Joseph and Paula can be seen as suffering
from anxiety: Joseph about his appearance, which may be
temporarily allayed by his decision to have cosmetic surgery,
and Paula about the fact that Joseph has 'humiliated' her. The
script in Chapter 6 (*see page 73*) can help someone who may
feel that they can't come up with a constructive solution for
anxiety symptoms on their own.

❖ ❖ ❖

Jeremy was a university graduate who had studied psychology and many alternative healing and meditation disciplines.
He was constantly looking for peace of mind, but could not
find it because he was plagued with an almost constant feeling of anxiety.

He had come to learn hypnotherapy as a profession and
was attending one of my courses. He said there were some
things in his past that he didn't want to deal with; they were too
horrible. He suffered hot sweats when he was nervous, sweaty
palms when he met new people, a perpetual feeling of inferior-
ity and lack of confidence, feelings of panic, and thoughts that
the world was too difficult and full of problems and he would
never be able to get it right. In fact he didn't enjoy his life at all.
Of course he would have good times, but he focused on the bad.

As the training course came to an end Jeremy realized
that he would have to access his early trauma in order to clear

the way for his future. He admitted prior to being regressed that he had been sexually abused at 12 years old. I didn't have to make him relive the experience while being regressed in hypnosis but he was able to look at it in a detached way. He was able to laugh at the fact that he'd been carrying this horrific experience around with him for most of his life. The hypnosis made him feel free of it. For the first time I saw a positive person with a life to look forward to.

❖ ❖ ❖

Deborah was a successful scriptwriter for television. She experienced exciting highs and then would be down in the dumps for days. She felt, she said, 'out of balance'. She 'coped' by drinking and eating excessively.

Things were coming to a head by the time she came to see me. She had always had a good relationship with her parents and had enjoyed her childhood, so she couldn't work out when this constant anxiety had first taken hold.

When she was regressed I found that she didn't feel loved. She tried to compensate for this by getting involved with a great many men, most of whom were completely wrong for her. And of course this made life even more complicated, taking a toll on her emotions and general health.

Together Deborah and I worked on visualizations (*see page 65*) to help improve her sense of worth. She was actually worried that this work might negatively affect her writing. In fact, once she was no longer burdened by anxiety her scripts became much more multi-faceted and compassionate.

People live (and sometimes die) with inner turmoil when it is so easily alleviated by some self-help or work with a hypnotherapist.

❖ ❖ ❖

Julian was under a great deal of stress when he came to see me. He had two daughters; one was brain damaged and the other had just developed stomach ulcers. He felt anxious all the time and could see no way out.

In this case the facts were that he had serious practical difficulties and responsibilities. Nevertheless, it's the way we deal with our problems that makes all the difference. Through his work with me he came to realize that he felt unable to show affection to anyone, including his wife and children, 'for his own protection' as he put it. He had lived in a battleground as a child; his parents were alcoholics and would also beat him.

Hypnosis allowed him to see the pain his wife and daughters felt at his seeming indifference. Over time he felt safe to allow himself to feel and react emotionally. He loved his wife and children deeply and now he was finally able to show it.

NOSTRIL BREATHING – A SIMPLE RELAXATION TECHNIQUE

Place your forefinger over your right nostril and press lightly to close the nostril. Now take a deep breath, inhaling through your left nostril. Think of your lungs filling up and expanding completely, imagine how they will look as they expand. Remove your finger from your right nostril and place it on your left nostril. Exhale fully and completely through your right nostril. Repeat 10 times.

As you are doing these exercises, it is always useful to give yourself some affirmation when you are in the relaxed state. An affirmation is a positive programming message for your brain, for example: 'I am at peace with myself and fully relaxed' or 'My heartbeat is calm and regular.'

MORE ANXIETY-RELEASING EXERCISES

Erickson was one of the revered master hypnotherapists of his day – NLP (Neuro Linguistic Programming) was developed from some of his teachings. He often used a crystal ball, a technique to encourage the imagination to bring forward useful information.

If you think that this method seems childish, I can assure you it is very sophisticated. Erickson used it to create extraordinary desired changes for his patients. It is just a tool to allow your inner mind to communicate with you in the form of fantasy, your inner mind language.

This exercise is meant to be used in hypnosis. It has little value if you try and think about it consciously, unless you are well practised in meditation or deep relaxation techniques. It is quite normal to wonder if you are 'in deep enough' to allow the exercise to work. Since there is no special feeling, just accept it. Worrying will just bring your conscious back. Just let it happen. Your conscious interference is wasting your time, so keep it in check. The fact that you will be using your mind's eye will ensure you are in a sufficient state of trance. Whenever you daydream you have already hypnotized yourself. It's part of your daily life.

> *Put yourself into relaxation with one of the inductions in Chapter 5 and then imagine that you have a crystal ball. Imagine in your mind's eye that you are gazing into the ball. Then imagine that your anxiety or problem has been resolved. Begin to ask yourself some pertinent questions: 'How did I get over my fear? How did I get so relaxed?' You can prompt yourself by imagining a fog. Tell yourself that the fog will soon start to dissipate by degrees; as this is happening allow yourself to discover some signposts that will give you clues on how you resolved the problem.*

After some practice, you can try another, similar exercise where you allow yourself to have three crystal balls. The first one shows you forgotten memories. This technique enables you to become an onlooker, observing yourself in certain difficult circumstances. This is called disassociation and allows you to look from an entirely different viewpoint. It also serves to create a pathway to provide some important memories that may help you to understand your dilemma.

The second crystal ball allows you to look at something that is likely to happen in the future when you are released and free from anxiety.

The third ball enables you to picture a role model, perhaps the face of someone you admire. It may be a TV personality or someone you know. You slip into their body, be them (you can easily do this in trance work). Then you let them voice their opinion about your situation and allow them to give you some advice. You may be surprised at what information comes forward.

When you are in trance, simply by allowing yourself to relax your mind is very focused and your imagination is far more fertile than normally. Imagination is the key to your inner mind – it is how your inner mind contacts you, giving you inspiration or warnings about yourself.

It would be wise to remember that every problem exists for a very good reason – they help us to grow and learn about ourselves. These simple techniques help you to start to change your own negative programming.

BODY FOCUSING

The following exercise was presented at a rather interesting talk I attended in France. It illustrates the close inter-relationship which Fitz Perls, another master of hypnosis, felt existed between the mind – expressed through thoughts, feelings and language – and the body. The body speaks a sort of language through gestures, posture and movement. You automatically decode the language of the body: this is how you can tell when someone is on their guard, happy, suspicious, etc.

First close your eyes and allow yourself to relax. The countdown method (see page 100) could be appropriate.
First, describe to yourself what you are experiencing. Then, change the descriptive inner dialogue. For

example: 'There is tension in my back' might be restated 'My back is tense,' then 'I am tensing my back.' Notice and focus on the sensations there. Wait for any associated thoughts, feelings and ideas. You might find that an image appears of being in a tense and difficult social situation, and handling it with restraint in spite of feeling annoyed. Intuition and ideas will usually pop into your mind when you are open to them. With practice, you learn to observe carefully whatever emerges or manifests itself.

A FUN EXERCISE

Get some large pieces of scrap paper and a pen. Ask yourself the following questions (no need to worry about grammar or spelling, as you have no need to show it to anyone):

If your life were a movie, what title would you give it? What would be the main theme? Drama, comedy, thriller? Describe it in one page.

Compose a short story entitled 'My Dream'. Just write it as fast as you can without thinking about it. Write one page.

Examine the two pages and see where they are similar. Are there aspects about your movie (i.e. your life) that you could change if you wanted to? Be very objective and critical. No excuses, no denial. There is no good or bad, you're just taking stock of your current situation.

Taking Stock of Yourself

Think about what you would be like without your anxieties, how would things change? Are you perhaps using your fear for some other purpose? How can you start to deal with the problem behind the fear? Add your thoughts about this to the end of your favourite relaxation script from Chapter 6.

Sometimes the mind is so powerful that the tricks it performs look like magic. Uri Geller's bending of spoons is a good example of this. If you are sceptical about how powerful the mind is, and worry about scientifically proven techniques, you should read the very interesting book *Mind Machines* by scientist Harry Stine. In this book he quotes Robert A. Heinlein: 'One man's magic is another man's technology.' He suggests that magic is a technology that we don't yet understand.

Certain responses can cause 'a mix-up in labelling': a person may believe they have one problem when in fact at heart lies another.

A client of mine called Steve believed he suffered from panic attacks. He had been to see psychiatrists, psychologists and support groups. He was unable to be desensitized to his condition because it could erupt at any time, anywhere.

During his earlier psychoanalysis, he had explained to the specialist that his mother had had polio. She had been taken to hospital for a long stay when he was three years old. All he could see when he went to visit her was her head. She even had a baby while she was still in the hospital.

The psychiatrist had felt that Steve was probably suffering intense anxiety stemming from the time when his mother had been taken been away from him. Steve, however, didn't buy this explanation. He remembered the first time that he had suffered an attack: He had been in a restaurant at a breakfast meeting. The only people there were colleagues whom he knew and felt quite comfortable with. However, he started to feel clammy, hot and a bit dizzy. He thought it was flu and after the meeting he went home. It started to subside when he was driving home, only to resume as he entered his house. He took his temperature and found it was extremely high and his heart was racing. A few days later when he was driving to work it started again. He had suffered these attacks repeatedly over the next 15 years.

In hypnotherapy with me he was regressed to when he was five years old. It was his first day at school. He arrived very early and was ushered into an empty classroom by a new teacher, and told to wait there. It was a big room and he was very scared. He didn't know what to do, so he went home. As he was walking home he felt even more scared. He knew the maid would be very angry. It transpired he had just been too early and there had been an oversight on the part of the teacher; she should have taken him personally into the class and waited with him there.

The next time he had a similar fear was when he was learning to read. His teacher had called him stupid. He knew he wasn't stupid and this made him very angry, also it embarrassed him in front of the class. The next experience was again in class, when the teacher picked on him for forgetting his homework. She took him to the head-teacher, who phoned his father.

This set of circumstances had created deep feelings of embarrassment and lack of self-esteem. So what Steve had always classified to himself as 'panic attacks' actually stemmed from deep-seated anxiety about his self-worth. When asked to re-examine the experience in the restaurant he realized that all the people at the breakfast were older than he. And though it was true that they were patting him on the back for having engineered a turn-around for their department since he had been put in to manage it, he felt he didn't deserve the credit, putting it down to luck rather than his own ability. The attention made him feel acutely embarrassed and brought back all the old negative feelings. Thus began his years of anxiety.

Steve was a trainee hypnotherapist and had helped other people with phobias, but that didn't make it any easier to help himself. With the work done in regression, he not only lost the fear but regained his confidence. In hypnosis Steve was asked to go down the line of fear to bring him to the very first time he felt it. This is how he came to the memory of the five-year-old at school.

These were, of course, fairly advanced techniques and Steve had the help of a skilled practitioner. But there are gentle self-hypnosis techniques that you can use to bypass anxiety. The crystal ball technique (*see page 47*) along with the appropriate suggestion from Chapter 6 will help you to overcome your problem. Many of the techniques mentioned in the next two chapters will also be of use, as will the specific Suggestion scripts for anxiety-related problems (*see pages 95–98 in Chapter 6*).

Four

PANIC ATTACKS

The difference between panic attacks and anxiety is that the panic attack is specific, while anxiety is more or less a constant state. Panic attacks are both more intense and less long-lasting than anxiety. And while a phobia can be traced to a distinct cause, panic attacks are usually less easily ascribed to a particular trigger.

❖ ❖ ❖

During a full-blown panic attack your body is put on alert, ready to fight or flee for your life – except there is no genuine need to do either, so you are left with your body's over-wrought responses. The lack of control as you feel your heart thumping only adds to the fear. The difference between a panic attack and a phobia is that you know what the phobia is about. It can be cats, horses, people. Although you may experience the same physical responses during a panic attack, you generally have no idea what has caused it. It can happen at any time, or so it seems.

Sometimes you are aware that there is a pattern to the attacks. If you always experience a panic attack on trains, then it could be said that you have a phobia of trains which creates the attack, but if you suddenly feel one coming on when you are out walking, and then again in the pub, drinking with friends, then you may start to feel the fear and helplessness that come from being afflicted with such an unpredictable and disabling condition.

THE SYMPTOMS

* Emotional distress
* Apprehension
* Alarm
* Severe physical discomfort
* Rapid heart rate
* Rapid breathing
* Diarrhoea
* Nausea
* Shaking
* Hot sweats
* Blotches
* Facial twitches

Panic attacks can foster certain negative emotional 'side-effects' as well, such as timidity, shyness, severe lack of confidence, feelings of inadequacy and, worst of all, the feeling of being unloved or unworthy.

My mother was a victim of valium in the early 1970s. This was when doctors weren't aware of how strong an addiction the drug created. They would give them out like sweets. My mother was bedridden and, unbeknown to us, she would send a taxi to collect another prescription from the doctor. It was later discovered that the side-effects could lead to agoraphobia, which she later suffered from, although at the time this condition wasn't recognized. My mother could remember walking down the street when she suffered what we know today as a panic attack. She was frightened she would pass out in the street. It gave her a shock and caused her to lose her confidence. She was scared and felt out of control, so she literally stopped going out. At first it wasn't too noticeable. She would make excuses to herself that she didn't need to go out. My father was only too glad to do the shopping and take care of her. She gradually became an invalid, just living on valium and sleeping pills. I have seen many clients who suffer from agoraphobia because of an initial panic attack. The good news is that it doesn't matter how many years you have suffered. You can be released from panic attacks.

Because you don't always understand what is causing a panic attack, the brain tries to fill in imaginary reasons or explanations for it. This serves only to cause frustration and fear for the victim. The phobia is different in the respect that the person knows that a fear of snakes, spiders or what have you is at the heart of their reaction. They do not start questioning their sanity, unlike the victim of the panic attack. It doesn't make too much difference in terms of treatment, but at least the phobic has something to go on and this makes it easier for them and for the hypnotherapist.

WHAT IS FEAR?

The amygdala is central to fear. When something happens that frightens you – for example if a noise wakes you from your sleep and another crash gives you the impression that there may be an intruder in the house – the amygdala acts like an alarm system.

When you first perceive the noise, the ear takes in the sound waves and sends them down a circuit to the brainstem and then to the thalamus (*see Figure*). Here two branches separate: a smaller bundle of projections lead to the amygdala and the nearby hippocampus, and a larger pathway leads to the auditory cortex in the temporal lobe, where sounds are sorted out and made sense of.

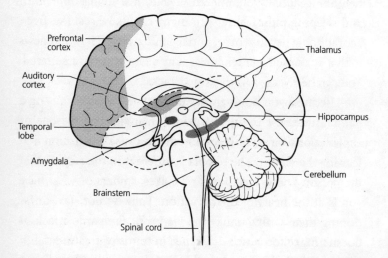

Fig 1: The alarm pathways of the brain

The hippocampus, which acts as a 'storage site' for the memory, immediately searches to see if the noise is a familiar one. While this is going on, the auditory cortex is analysing the sound to try to understand the source, checking all the possibilities in a flash. If the sound is familiar, then it stops there. If not, another coil of circuitry reverberates between the amygdala, hippocampus and prefrontal cortex. If there is no satisfying explanation after further analysis, then the amygdala triggers an alarm to the nervous system. It works similarly to those home alarm systems where operators stand at the ready to send out calls to the local police or fire department. And just as each of these departments has a different job to do, so have the different elements of the nervous system. Each sensory system is checked and the body's emergency impulses, which mobilize the fight-or-flight response, are now in action. All this happens in seconds, resulting, in some people, in an acute panic attack.

John came to me suffering from severe panic attacks. He was in his early twenties, smart and nice looking and financially secure. Yet when I asked him how much joy he had in his life his answer was 'zero.' He said that recently his drinking had been getting out of control. When drunk he would become quite violent, so he had resolved that the time had come to do something about it.

He regularly suffered extreme panic attacks. They prevented him from going out with his friends. He would either drink beforehand to work up the courage to go out or, more often than not, he would just stay in. He was becoming very introverted and his work was

also suffering. In fact, he found it difficult to go to work
at all and kept making excuses to stay home.

　　When I talked to him some more, I learned that his
father had been a violent and abusive alcoholic. He used
to bash the doors down to get in the house when he was
locked out. John was horrified of the violence and hated
it. Yet when things got bad he imitated his father's
behaviour.

　　In regression he was taken to the first time he had
had a panic attack. He was five years old. His father was
being taken away by the police. John felt very sick and
nearly blacked out with fear.

　　After therapy, the panic attacks came less severe.
He was going whole days without experiencing one,
which hadn't been the case for years, and he was starting
to revert back to his naturally happy-go-lucky self.

Because panic attacks are usually linked to extreme anxiety,
let's look at what makes us anxious. When we move out of our
'comfort state', beyond the familiar and known, we all of us
feel a certain amount of apprehension and anxiety. The triggers of a panic attack can also be cumulative, making it difficult to uncover the causes behind them. Relationship worries,
stress at work and other variables can all combine to produce
panic attacks.

　　For example, a colleague of mine had a client who was
a white South African who had grown up in Johannesburg.
She had never seen the real poverty that existed only a mile
down the road from her home. Her small, insulated commu-
nity was her comfort zone. When she moved to the UK she felt

extremely anxious whenever she saw examples of poverty on TV or on the street, when around black people, or indeed whenever she encountered something beyond the range of her former experience. Although at first it seemed that each of these anxieties would have to be dealt with individually, the answer lay in handling them collectively, as they were an accumulation of fears springing from her deep sense of unease and guilt at the heart of being raised in such an unjust and divisive society. Someone else who had moved out of their 'safe area' could have found the experience liberating and exciting because they hadn't suffered the traumatic experience that had served to created such suffering in her case.

❖ ❖ ❖

As mentioned earlier, sometimes a build-up of negative emotions about yourself and life in general can lead to generalized panic attacks. In Chapter 6 you will find Suggestion scripts that deal with helping yourself to combat stress, anger and grief and improve your self-confidence and assertiveness.

Five

SELF-HYPNOSIS TECHNIQUES

An American hypnotherapist said in frustration to the client who thought hypnosis was sleep, 'If you're not aware of what's happening you're probably dead.'

❖ ❖ ❖

Hypnosis is a state of altered consciousness that happens to everyone. Just before you go to sleep you are in this day-dreamy state. In hypnotherapy you are guided into this state and the state is prolonged by suggestion. You are not asleep. When you are in hypnosis you are awake, therefore you are aware of everything that is going on. If you are asleep you cannot be in hypnosis.

Hypnosis can be used to overcome a wide range of problems, including smoking, overweight, learning difficulties, fear of public speaking, stress, panic attacks, fear of flying and all phobic fears, emotional problems, compulsive behaviour, bed-wetting and many more. And hypnosis is not just a formula to help you with your problems; it is also a positive therapy that can help you improve your whole life: to be more confident, more positive, happier, better in business, or for immediate improvement at your favourite sport or learning to speed read in one hour. It allows you instantaneously to improve without the usual repetition or practice that is normally necessary to learn (or unlearn) any habit.

IS HYPNOSIS DANGEROUS?

Absolutely not. When you see certain stage hypnotists you may feel that the subjects are in danger of looking foolish, but even then they are always capable of bringing themselves out of hypnosis, just as they could bring themselves out of any daydream. I know – I have done just that, because I came out of hypnosis when I didn't want to do what I was asked. But this didn't stop me being re-hypnotized by the same stage hypnotist to do other antics and thoroughly enjoying the experience. It is always your choice.

This chapter has been designed to give you a simple guide on how to hypnotize yourself, or you can ask a partner or trusted friend to help. If you prefer to work and create your own therapy, I have listed the instructions and tools for you to do this. But first you may be a little unsure of what hypnosis is. The following questions and answers are ones I come across most frequently.

WHAT IS HYPNOSIS?

Hypnosis is a state of mind that we all experience. It has been equated with the moment we wake in the morning or just before we drift off into sleep. We exit the hypnotic state to allow us to enter sleep, but the transition is so subtle we are unaware when it happens. If you have experienced a daydream you have been in a form of hypnosis.

CAN ANYONE BE HYPNOTIZED?

Considering all hypnosis is self-hypnosis and everyone has daydreams, the answer has to be 'yes.' The exception to the rule is the person with brain damage or one with a total breakdown in concentration; although in my view, this type of person is constantly in a natural hypnotized state – a permanent daydream. I have never failed in my practice to hypnotize someone who wanted to be hypnotized.

If you don't want to be hypnotized, you won't be. You can stop the procedure by refusing to accept the hypnotic instructions by forcing other thoughts in. This may be difficult – it's a bit like letting the door-to-door salesman into your home and trying *not* to buy from him. His whole professionalism is based on talking you round. He does it day in and day out, so he is going to know all your get-outs and find ways to use them to his advantage.

One of the hurdles to self-hypnosis is that because there is no great change that you feel when in hypnosis (just as there is no great change in how you feel when you are daydreaming), it can be difficult to know when you are hypnotized. The only difference is that you will feel completely relaxed.

The exception to this may be if something you have read or heard about hypnosis has taken hold in your subconscious, in which case you might experience some feeling or a tingling sensation, which the subconscious 'expects' to feel when you are in hypnosis.

The other hurdle to be overcome is that some people worry that they are not 'visually orientated' enough to work through the visualizations and suggestions that go hand in hand with hypnosis. You can test how visual you are just by closing your eyes and imagining a chair. Look and see what colour your chair is, then look to see what it is made of. Open your eyes and ask yourself if you saw the chair in your mind's eye or whether you just 'knew' what it looked like. If you saw what it looked like, then you are a visual person. Sigmund Freud, from his extensive study on hypnosis, estimated that two-thirds of us are visual and the other third are not. I am not. I am the type of person who until recently hypnotherapists thought were difficult or even impossible to hypnotize. Some highly qualified professionals and even top psychiatrists believe this still. Just remember this: no matter how your brain works, you can still imagine things in your own way. Because I had this problem, I have devised a method so that the non-visual among us can be put into hypnosis easily. As you did with the chair, if I say 'Picture in your mind...' then do it in your own way or mentally swap the word 'picture' for 'imagine' or 'imagine you can picture ...'

SHALL I BE AWARE
OF WHAT'S HAPPENING?

Yes! Most people feel surprised that they don't feel any different while they are in hypnosis, just relaxed. Afterwards, when you come out of hypnosis, you realize how relaxed you have been. When you are in hypnosis you are still aware of what is happening around you and your subconscious is more keen. Therefore, all your senses are sharper. This is very easy to prove.

Imagine you are driving down a motorway, one you are very familiar with. You may start to go into a daydream, thinking what you will be doing when you get to your destination. You go into a type of auto-pilot state, oblivious to your surroundings. You can be in this state of daydream for a few minutes. When you come out of this trance-type daydream, you may realize that you haven't even noticed the scenery or what cars are on the road and look quickly to see if there are any police about and that you are not speeding. You may even think that if you had not come out of this state you could have had an accident. In fact, when your conscious is occupied in this state of trance, the subconscious part of your mind comes forward as a protection mechanism. Your subconscious heightens your senses, so that they are more aware. If the car in front of you had put his brake lights on while you were in your daydream, you would have immediately been fully alert, in control and dealing with the situation.

This incredibly sophisticated programme we take for granted and don't even notice, but it is at the very essence of hypnosis. When you are in hypnosis you are protected by this very programme and so, if anything untoward happens while you are in the daydream state, then because your senses are so keen you will immediately terminate the trance. This is why hypnosis is so safe.

SO I AM NOT ASLEEP THEN?

No! Under no circumstances. But you may look fast asleep to the onlooker and that is where the confusion lies.

I remember being in my rooms in Harley Street, working with the chairman of the board of a very large corporate company and he was so deep in hypnosis he was slumped in the chair. When he came out of this particularly deep trance, he remarked: 'I wasn't in hypnosis, but I wasn't asleep either.' Sadly, I didn't have the video equipment I have now, otherwise I could have shown him that he had indeed been in hypnosis!

IS THERE ANY CAUSE FOR CONCERN?

If you are using self-hypnosis, then there is none. Unfortunately, the press have publicized cases of misconduct involving hypnotherapists that leave a question mark in this area. What I *can* say is that registers exist to regulate all qualified hypnotherapists. If you have any doubts about the methods used by a hypnotherapist you are thinking of seeing, then do check that they are registered.

If drugs are used with hypnosis, then there is certainly a possible cause for concern. But you can be assured that responsible hypnotherapists never use drugs as part of their treatment, and normal (i.e. drug-less) hypnosis techniques cannot be responsible for you doing anything against your moral, political or religious beliefs.

SO HOW DO YOU HYPNOTIZE YOURSELF?

In order to hypnotize yourself (or someone else) you need to follow three basic steps:

1   Induction script (*see pages 73–94*)
    ('Deepeners' [*see page 94*) can be used before the
    suggestion for deeper relaxation)
2   Suggestion scripts (as found in Chapters 6 and 7)
3   Counting out of hypnosis (*see page 71 in Chapter 5*)

The Induction script is a selection of words used to induce the hypnosis. There are three types of induction used to relax a person into hypnosis. In order of extremes they are the instant induction, rapid induction and the progressive induction.

Instant Induction

The instant induction, which has a shock element and is immediate, looks very impressive for demonstrations, taking only seconds to induce full relaxation. It can be as dramatic as the hypnotist grabbing a subject by the head, shoulders or arms and barking out the order: 'Sleep!'

Instant induction is used mainly by hypnotists in the US and is quite spectacular to witness. The subject may look as if he has gone into a faint but is fully aware and finds it pleasant and relaxing. It is very effective, demonstrating the power of suggestion at its best. If a person has experienced a severe trauma or scare, he or she will be automatically in hypnosis. The conscious mind stops processing and the subconscious is vulnerable. This induction needs another person to act as hypnotist and cannot be used for self-hypnosis.

Rapid Induction

The rapid induction, which basically confuses the mind, over-loading it, presents a more gentle approach but still takes less than a minute to induce.

The American Dave Elman, a modern master of hypnosis, has developed a method of rapid induction which uses confusion and complicated short instructions to close down the conscious part of the mind, thus exposing the subconscious. It is very effective and this type of induction is useful for inducing hypnosis once a person has already experienced hypnosis before. As with instant induction, this method needs another to perform the hypnosis and so is unsuitable for self-hypnosis.

Progressive Induction

The progressive induction really bores the mind into hypnosis. It is considered the most reliable and is the method most usually used for self-hypnosis. You need not have another person present to guide you into hypnosis; you can just listen to a recording, either bought or pre-recorded by yourself.

The progressive inductions provided in this book (*see pages 73–94*) range in length from approximately 3 to 12 minutes, depending on which you choose and how slowly you talk. It is best to talk in a gentle, monotonous voice, slightly highlighting the words that you find important to you. If you are taping the suggestions, talk much more slowly than you would in normal conversation.

❖ ❖ ❖

The induction scripts are the words used to encourage the hypnotic state. Inductions act like a mind massage, massaging away problems and filtering into the subconscious mind. You begin with an induction script and then add the suggestion of your choice. It is as simple as that. You can choose an induction script that takes you by the sea, into a garden, on a boat or on a magical journey. To help you read the scripts aloud with the correct pauses, I have purposely exaggerated the spacing (shown by ellipses: …… in the scripts). It is also important to realize that this is one of those rare instances where your grammar and syntax do not have to be precise. In fact, it may be to your advantage if the words are not arranged with complete accuracy, as this causes a controlled confusion of your mind, leading you more easily into relaxation.

About the Suggestion Scripts

The suggestion scripts are a set of instructions to the subconscious mind, creating and persuading change. You will find many scripts to choose from in Chapter 6, along with some pointers for designing your own. Since you just need to record them onto a cassette recorder and then play the tape back to yourself, you can find it not only easy but most enjoyable. But be careful – since your mind will only accept positive changes in hypnosis, you are in danger of becoming very happy!

To Terminate the Trance

You never need worry about coming out of a trance. You will come out naturally, or even instantly, if there are things that need to be attended to, like the telephone ringing or someone at the door. Otherwise you can use a counting out method (*see page 71*). Note, hypnosis is a heightened state of awareness rather than sleep, so you are likely to notice any exterior noises more than you would normally, just as you would as you were going to sleep. You do not need silence for trance, but you need to be somewhere comfortable, warm and ideally where you will not be interrupted.

Counting Out of Hypnosis

You can choose to count out of hypnosis by using whatever combination of numbers you prefer. I like to count out from 10 backwards to 1. If you want to use your self-made tape as an aid to getting to sleep, then you can either choose to ignore the counting out part of the tape or you can just leave it out completely. If you are finding that you go to sleep quickly, that too is OK. As long as you have heard the tape through once, the mind will use it as a trigger.

It is wise to use the suggestions each day or evening for three weeks to establish the habit. Just as you wake up or go to bed is an ideal time if you never seem to have enough time in

the day. But remember: this may be why you need the tape in
the first place – because you never leave yourself enough time
to relax!

> *In a moment I will count from 10 to 1......and at the*
> *count of 1 you will open your eyes......and feel fully*
> *aware and enthusiastic......10, 9, 8......coming up*
> *now......7, 6, 5......more and more aware......4, 3,*
> *2, 1......eyes open.*

Accessing Your Subconscious in Self-hypnosis: A Little Mind Exercise

This exercise can be applied if you wish to ask questions of
your subconscious while you are in self-hypnosis, when you
reach your special place, a place you choose to be. It could be
in the middle of one of the inductions. Include a long space in
your tape recording for you to work on yourself. During this
pause on the tape, imagine a TV screen about 1 metre high
and pose questions to it. Imagine that the TV screen is your
subconscious – whatever thought comes immediately into
your mind, either onto the screen or just as a word, that is the
answer from your subconscious. Don't analyse the answer. At
first, practise with simple questions like: 'Why am I having
trouble sleeping?' or 'Why am I getting so many colds?'

Learn to trust the answers from your subconscious.

Six

SELF-HYPNOSIS SCRIPTS

Suggestions are the key to your future happiness.

❖ ❖ ❖

This chapter is dedicated to the Induction and Suggestion scripts which can relax you into that wonderful state in which you can change your habits, behaviour and negative thought-patterns. The first section of this chapter includes a large selection of inductions. The next section is the suggestions you use while you are in hypnosis. The words used are ones to instruct your mind for change. Some are specific and others are general.

INDUCTION SCRIPTS

The Induction is the words used to persuade the conscious to relax and quieten, to allow the subconscious mind to have the floor.

You can use the scripts below by asking someone to read to you or by taping them on a recorder and playing them back to yourself. Your tape should begin with a progressive relaxation Induction (*pages 74-94*) and be followed by the appropriate Suggestion (*pages 74–94*), then end with the counting out of hypnosis (*page 71*). When you are recording the tape, use a slow, monotonous tone of voice for the Induction, and a more enthusiastic style for the Suggestion. The count out of hypnosis should be done in a strong and forceful voice, still maintaining the enthusiasm.

Be sure that you are sitting or lying down comfortably as you listen to the script you have chosen. Uncross your legs, let your arms fall naturally at your sides and make sure your neck is supported.

Relaxation Induction Script

The following is a very good first-time Induction script, but you will find a great variety selected for different individuals. For example, someone with a highly refined visual sense will prefer flowery descriptive scripts, while someone else will prefer scripts that are short and to the point. Just choose which you prefer or try them all out to suit your mood at any given time.

> *I want you to imagine that you're checking your body to ensure you become totally relaxed......as your muscles relax, just let your mind relax also......begin with your feet......feel your toes......stretch them......feel the texture of what your feet are resting*

on...begin to tighten your calves......now relax them......let that relaxation spread past your ankles ......up your calves to the back of your knee......feel those muscles easing......resting comfortably...... now your thighs......pull them tight......be aware of those long muscles tensing......now relax those muscles......feel them lengthening and resting comfortably......feel your legs as they sink even deeper into the cushions as you relax even more......now your stomach muscles......pull them together gently ......now let them expand and relax comfortably.

Your shoulders and back muscles......flex your shoulders......feel those muscles pull across your back......now let your shoulders slouch as you relax the muscles......and notice how your spine sinks deeper into your chair, as you relax even more deeply......notice how easy and regular your breathing has become.

Now your fingertips and fingers......clench them......feel that tension......now relax them...... and allow the relaxation to spread up your arms to your neck. Make sure your neck is comfortable, with your head in an easy position......tighten up your neck muscles......now let them loosen up......as the muscles relax, allow your neck to shrink into the cushions into a comfortable position.

Your face muscles are flat and stretch comfortably across your face......squeeze up your face and feel the tension......now relax those muscles and feel them lengthening and softening......relaxing...... more than ever before.

You can now feel the air temperature against your skin......it feels smooth and comfortable...... now you can allow the relaxation to spread to your scalp......knowing that you are relaxed throughout your body......from the top of your head......to the tips of your toes.

Your body is now loose......and limp......and heavy......and relaxed......notice how your body is sinking deeper into relaxation......as your breathing becomes more regular and easy......in a moment I will count slowly from 1......to 10......and with each number you drift......deeper......and deeper...... into peaceful relaxation. 1......2......3......4......5 ......6......7......8......9......10 [count slowly and deliberately].

You are now feeling so deeply relaxed......you find it easy to focus your attention......and imagine things very clearly......and I want you to imagine that you are standing on a balcony......which has steps leading down to a beautiful garden......as you look into the garden......you see that it is surrounded with lovely trees......ensuring the garden is private......secluded and peaceful......there are flower beds set in the lovely lawn......and further along is a waterfall......flowing into a stream......listen to the sound of the water......as you look around, you see the trees......and you hear a faint sound of a bird in the distance......adding to the feeling of deep...... relaxation......through your entire being.

If you look more closely you will see that there are five steps leading down to the garden......and then a small path......that leads to the waterfall......in a moment we will walk down the steps......and with each step you go deeper......and deeper......into relaxation......so let's begin.

Watch your foot as you place it onto the first step......and as you do this you feel yourself going deeper into relaxation......down onto the second step......and as you feel your foot firmly placed on the step......you feel a wonderful relief......as you drift even deeper into relaxation......down onto the third step......feeling wonderfully free and......so......so ......relaxed. As your foot reaches for the fourth step......another wave of relaxation drifts through your whole body......down onto the fifth step now......and feeling even more deeply relaxed than ever before.

Now you are standing on the lawn......you see a little way ahead......the waterfall......and at the side of it is a garden bench......notice the colour of the bench......what it is made of......in a moment I would like you to walk over to the bench......and sit down on the bench......when you sit down you will be surprised at how comfortable it is......and then you will be even more relaxed than you are now......so let's begin to walk over......now sit down on the bench......and as you sit down on the bench......take a deep breath......and as you breathe out......you feel a wave of relaxation go through your body......relaxing every muscle and nerve......as you breathe in......you breathe in positive thoughts ......and as you breathe out......you breathe out negative thoughts......leaving room for more positive thoughts.

There follow eight gentle Inductions. The basic ideas for them have come from some of my wonderfully intuitive students from all over the world.

Bubbles

Imagine that you live in a simple village......life is very calm......and......contented......a comfortable existence. You are washing clothes at the river in front of your house......Your house is a hand-built wooden construction......perfect for the climate......on this beautiful tropical island. It is a balmy, sunny day......the breeze makes you feel so comfortable......You are washing your clothes, so relaxing......every time you finish washing a piece of clothing......you put it in the river to rinse it clean......the flow of the river water gently passes through your fingers......passes through the clothes ......and you feel so......so......relaxed......more relaxed......when feeling the flow of the river......

You see the bubbles appear from the flow of the river......the bubbles become bigger and bigger as you watch......They rise out of the water and float away......and as they do......you notice they get bigger and bigger......They expand......as you watch

*them float up......and up......into the sky. The more
they expand the more relaxed you become......You
put all your stress and problems into the bubbles......As they float away you notice how they dissi-
pate into the atmosphere......safe and no longer a
part of you......replaced with positive thoughts......
as you allow yourself to relax......*

*More and more bubbles appear......you are sur-
rounded by gentle bubbles and you know that all your
stress and anxiety have been swept away......The
feeling is so good and free......You can play with the
bubbles......put everything you don't want into the
bubbles......all the negative and mixed-up emotions
that are of no use to you......and the bubbles will carry them away.*

*You feel so free......you can now ask a question
which you would really like to know the answer
to......it may be a problem you need a solution
to......You may want direction......put your questions in the bubbles......The bubbles float higher and
higher......growing bigger and bigger......and when
they reach the top of the sky......they burst......
words fall from the bubbles......and as they fall the
words form a sentence. You are surprised to note the
sentence is the answer to your question......the
answer may surprise you......But you now realize it
makes sense.*

*One of the bubbles bursts......it is like a shower
falling down from the sky......It drops into your hand
but you don't notice it......on the way back from the*

river......you realize there is something in your hand. It is a token......you open your hand slowly......you look at the token......and an understanding flows through you like a wave of relaxation. All the old doubts, fears and problems which have bothered you just seem to float away and you feel so refreshed......and free.

Alone ... and Comfortable

Image you are planning for a retreat......away from the busy and hectic pace of life......and away from the family......You decide to go to an abandoned chalet at the edge of the jungle beside a waterfall......you feel safe and comfortable, as this is in your imagination a safe haven. You see the most beautiful sunset......It overlooks the mountains. The weather is a comfortable cool......soothing......a gentle breeze relaxing you......you experience a wonderful, fulfilling feeling of peace.

You walk towards a waterfall and lie down on the thick carpet of grass. You feel the water sprinkling your body......making you feel more refreshed and alive......Within a few moments you fall into a deep ......deep......sleep......While sleeping you dream that you are in a cave, lit at the far end by natural light spilling through a large hole in the rock......you feel so comfortable and your mind is so clear you realize that all your problems are small and that you can easily solve them by being constructive......Your mind is so ordered and clear that solutions come to *you easily......some are surprising and others are just common sense. You wake up from your dream and as you relax on the grass you realize how life can be so easy......you make the decision to enjoy your life and stop making it so complicated. You relax with this thought and drift into a comfortable place.*

Beach Fantasy

Allow yourself to imagine you are lying on a large beach towel......It is the height of summer and you are lying on soft luxurious golden sands in the middle of a beautiful beach......You can feel the infinite fineness of the sand below......moving to accommodate you in the most comfortable position you can imagine......While you lie there feeling totally relaxed ......soaking up the strong beating sun like liquid gold through your pores, you look around at the majestic scenery around you......The beach stretches out to the horizon in a gentle curve, the water lapping gently at its edges......Gliding up the foreshore and gliding back out......in tune with your peaceful breathing......With each breath you watch the lapping waves and feel doubly more relaxed. Heat shimmers off the golden sand......the only life a lonely sandpiper making its way across its sandy desert......You notice far down the beach a flash as something catches the sun......Curious, you gently rise and make your way down the beach......Your feet sink deeply into the warm sand with every step only increasing your sense of well-being and relaxation.

You head towards the top of the beach where sand dunes form tiny hills like scale mountains......As you wind between the windswept dunes you start to notice the vegetation start to increase as you travel......Sparse tundras turn to carpets of buffalo grass, which in turn become interspersed with sculptured shrubs looking like miniature bonsai laid out by an ancient Japanese gardener......As you rise above a crest......trees start to come into view...... lining the valley walls with thick green. Gnarled trunks form impossible contortions......creating the impression of a frenzied dance that was captured at its peak. The overhanging canopies of fervent green leaves cast shimmering patterns of speckled sunlight as you pass into the cool shadows heading down an old worn path......The path looks disused, as the underbrush has started to tentatively encroach upon it......You are filled with peace and calm as you continue deeper into the valley......Native plants become more numerous......ferns stretch from the ground and moss climbs laboriously up the trunks of nearby trees......Pleasant sounds start to insinuate themselves into your consciousness......Insects hum happily and a pair of tiny birds shrill sweetly as they dart between the branches of the nearest tree......You notice that the trees are wide and as you walk among them you enjoy the comfortable sensation of being perfectly at home......as these trees have been for centuries......The air seems fresh and moist, and you hear the distant sound of trickling water......You feel totally secure as you wander along the track......taking time to smell the multitude of smells that drift past your nose......and taking in the thousands of varieties of fauna......that seem to crowd around you each species......seeming to clamour to be looked at and examined.

As you walk......you begin to hear the sound of water increasing......a pleasant rhythmic pounding......that relaxes you with each step you take...... closer and closer......You round a corner and peer between two fronds at a magnificent sight......There in front of you, rising high above you......so that you can't see its top......is a gigantic waterfall......Seven cascades of water......plummet downward into a perfectly circular rock pool at your feet......The sound fills your ears and vibrates gently through your body, sending wave after wave of relaxation, as you stand there......feasting on the view......The water is absolutely clear......allowing you to see its smooth rocky bottom......Its lichen-covered surface forming a natural bowl......As you look at the rocks behind the foaming water......you see the glistening surface speckled with bright gold flecks......and realize what you had noticed flashing in the sun earlier......The water is cool and inviting so you move slowly into the rock pool, feeling the water rise past your feet and up to your ankles......cooling and numbing your skin gently......so that you hardly feel them at all......As you move deeper......the pleasant numbness spreads up your legs and over your waist......You allow yourself to drift into the water......floating on your back......all of your body numb now......you can hardly feel your body at all......You lie there absolutely comfortable......completely relaxed, just enjoying the sense of well-being and peace that flows through you.

The Island Fantasy

Now I want you to come on a journey of exploration. Imagine yourself on a tropical island where the sea is crystal clear and the colour of aquamarine......All around the island are lush green rainforests rising to magnificent heights that almost reach the clouds......Just outside your hotel is a small stream with a rustic wooden bridge across it......You cross the stream and listen to the trickling sound of the water flowing past smooth round pebbles and rocks......There is a clear path in front of you that leads into the rainforest. As you walk deeper into the rainforest......the tropical foliage above you...... shades you from the hot sun......and you notice a cool refreshing breeze......caressing your skin......All around you the soothing sounds of crickets......and birds singing......which fill the perfumed air...... Soon you turn a corner......and come to a sign that says......'This Way to the Wisdom Hermitage'...... you follow the arrows that are spaced evenly...... every ten steps on the path which winds up the mountain side in a spiral......you reach the top of the mountain and you see a cave in front of you......You know that you have reached the Wisdom Hermitage......and inside the cave......lives a wise old man whom you realize......you have come to see.

Just outside the cave you see two large rocks with a very smooth and flat surface facing each other. You sit down on the rock facing the cave and soon the wise old man comes out of the cave......He has the most gentle......kind......and loving......face. His eyes twinkle with great benevolence and he bids you welcome. You now ask him a question. He then hands you a gift which he places in your hand. You close your hand over the gift......thank him and say goodbye......You turn to walk back down the path you came along, and as soon as you turn a corner you open your hands and look at your gift. You pause and allow the meaning of the gift to seep through your whole being and you feel the wonderful comfort of understanding......you relax deeper and deeper into peaceful sleep.

Voyage of Discovery

Let yourself relax and allow the whole of your body to feel the wave of relaxation passing through you as you breathe more and more rhythmically......you are ready to go on a voyage of discovery......

You have been told that there is a very old temple......that will bring enlightenment to those who sit in it......but you were not told how to get there...... The only thing you were told was that you will only find it if you have truth in your heart......So you find *yourself walking along a path into fields......a gentle cool breeze is blowing.*

The path leads into a forest......and walking at your own pace......following the path amongst the trees......you see the dappled sunlight.

You come to a clearing and you see a wall in front of you......The path leads right past the wall......and you follow it......finding a way past the wall to continue on your journey......Beyond the wall......you see the most magnificent view you have ever seen......it makes you have a feeling that you have not felt since you were a young child.

Continuing on your journey......you pass the most beautiful scenery......trees and flowers so beautiful and colourful......You realize how lucky you are to be able to take the time to appreciate the wonder of nature......you have been so busy lately......too busy to look at what is around you......The simplicity and wonder of life itself......As you notice your surroundings you drift deeper and deeper into a peaceful relaxation.

Take a deep breath and allow yourself to relax all your body......from the top of your head to the bottom of your feet......Allow every muscle to relax comfortably......In a moment you can use your imagination to allow you to relax even more......I want you to visualize that you are flying like a bird up towards the sky......As you look down you can see a wonderful view......a village......a forest......and beyond an exquisite white sandy beach. Children are playing......they run around laughing......You can hear their voices clearly......the happy voices......as you glide across the sky.

Suddenly you see a little girl......alone......her face is full of sorrow......She looks up at you flying in the sky......Her eyes fill with hope......and she smiles.

Far away......groups of birds are flying very peacefully towards you......You allow your mind to relax......see how the birds are so easy as they glide along......you think about the little girl and remember when you were young......how all problems seemed so intense......now you are grown up you realize that you have choices......because you are an adult you can start to use new strategies to make your life easier......the wonderful thing is that you don't even need to try......you can just instruct your inner mind to do this......while you are getting on with your life......and the result is that you have better ideas......better ways to cope with everyday problems and ways to deal with them......in such a way......that the way you deal with them...... decreases your stress instead of adding to it.

The birds fly towards you and you notice that one of the birds drops something from its mouth...... This lands in front of the little girl......you can see quite clearly as you gently swoop down that it is a puzzle......The little girl picks the gift up and skips away happily......you realize that this is all that life is......a fascinating, wonderful puzzle......and you

*realize that you no longer need to take it so very seri-
ously as you have in the past......that you can easily
overcome any obstacles that come along. You are a
winner in the game of life......and the best thing
is you don't even have to compete. As you relax and
take a luxurious deep breath you feel very contented
and happy.*

Journey to Atlantis

*Imagine yourself at the top of a cliff top overlooking a
panoramic view of rugged coastline and emerald
sea......As you look down, you see a path winding
down towards the shore line......Although the path
is steep and is overgrown with spartan trees, the way
seems clear......You start down the path and as you
take your first few steps downhill......the next
foothold seems to rise up in front of you as if by magic......illuminating the way. The further downward
you descend the more relaxed you feel......Every step
becomes more natural to you as the track winds its
way through rocky outcrops and wind-sculptured
trees.*

*As you walk between two large boulders you find
yourself in a natural shrine within the rocks......A
mandala has been lovingly inscribed into the rock
face, and a small cairn at its foot is decorated in flowers and small offerings from past travellers......You
notice a small cave to one side, where a soft bed of
straw has been laid out......and you see that anyone
who wishes may use this place to rest. Although you*

could easily stop and spend the night here, you decide to continue down towards the shoreline below.

You continue down the path feeling more......and more......relaxed as you approach the bottom of the cliff......The rock path soon gives way to luxuriously soft sand and you feel your feet sink up to their ankles......as you make your way onto level ground......The sand becomes firm as you cross naturally-formed rocks to a beautiful rugged coastline lapped by crystal-clear azure waters.

You feel so relaxed and the water looks so inviting that you cannot resist removing your clothing......after filling your lungs with the fresh salt air......you dive deep into the water......As you enter the water you are surprised at how light you feel......The water is so clear you can see the sea floor heading further......and further down towards something that glimmers in the distance......Without thinking about it you immediately head in the direction of the faint glow......It comes as no surprise that you find it easy to breathe......in fact it hardly seems necessary to breathe at all......As you are drawn to the glow below you, you realize it is coming from inside a giant oyster......On reaching the oyster you see that the glow is caused by a huge pearl sitting at the back of the oyster......Instinctively you are drawn inside the oyster, immediately feeling totally relaxed as you enter and settle on the infinitely soft surface of the oyster's tongue......As you lie down you gaze into the roof of the oyster above you. It is a perfectly smooth mirror surface of mother-of-pearl and you see yourself reflected in it.

As you lie there feeling completely at home you become aware of someone else nearby......Sitting up, you see a beautiful mermaid floating above the pearl......bathed in its light......Without any words being spoken you realize you can ask any question of this vision and she will give you an answer. So you ask her your question......

As she gives you her answer she reaches into the pearl and hands you something that you know will help you......With infinite ease she glides off into the darkness and you suddenly feel a gentle pull......calling you towards the surface. In your own time you drift gently back to the surface of the water and climb back onto the rocks......Enjoying the warmth of sun soaking into you......you make your way leisurely back up the hill to the shrine you passed earlier and settle down on the bed of straw......With a smile of satisfaction you fall deeply and beautifully into sleep.

A Fairy Story

Imagine you are at the bottom of a steep hill with deep crevices......you are looking high into the sky......as you look far away......so......so high......you realize there is a clearing in the rocks......you notice a path of stone that slowly starts to ascend the high crevices ......you move to the clearing......you see a pair of walking shoes......hanging from a tree with a sign. You read the sign......it says 'put me on'. You look around to see if there is anybody there……but of course there is no one around……You glance back at the sign and it has now changed……it says 'Yes, you, take off your shoes and put these on.' As you change and put these new shoes on, they feel so comfortable……like slippers……and you realize your old shoes were not the right shoes for the climb and would have restricted you from getting to the top of the hill.

You feel stronger, as if the new shoes have some energy of their own. You start to walk up the clearing……and slowly start to walk up the hill……as you climb you notice some rocks and see some small flowers growing in the crevices……You are amazed at how the flowers are curled around the rocks…… You climb easily up past the rocks and the flowers……as you do you notice the beautiful colours and wonder at the beauty of the simple things that nature has to offer……You notice that your heart is beating calmly and comfortably as you climb……No need to rush……time is on your side.

You reach the first ledge with ease……you see a bubbling spring……you kneel down and drink…the water tastes wonderful……You drink deep and long……you sit up and rest while you take a look around to admire the view……as you look round you see a beautiful staff of carved wood. You pick up the staff and carry on up the mountain. The climb is much easier with this walking stick……You continue the journey up……you want to look back. You feel very comfortable as you see the valley below and, as

you look, questions about your life come to mind......
as you reach the top you see a sign that reads 'Echo
Point'......you turn and look at the valley below and
you have an urge to shout something......to your surprise you shout out a question......You consider the
question that you shout and realize it is very important to you......You put your hand to your ear and to
your surprise an answer comes back......You sit and
rest and ponder the answer......You close your eyes
for a moment and when you open them you find you
are back where you started at the bottom of the
hill......But you find that this is a relief......the climb
has served its purpose......you now understand how
easy it is to climb and it is your choice whether to do
so or not......and if you do decide to do the climb
again you can also choose how you would like to go.

Still in the countryside......enjoying the great
outdoors......You find yourself crossing a field planted with wheat......The wheat is swaying and swish-
ing in the gentle breeze......You are enjoying the
feeling of being alone......at one with nature......

At the end of the path......a country road with
fields either side and the sun warm on your
back......You have no idea where you will end up but
you are happy and enjoying the stroll......at one with
the Universe.

At the end of the path you follow the road off to
the left......clearly marked 'The Grotto'......you are
curious as to the meaning of the word 'grotto'......but
you know that they are magical places.

At the end of this road is a small grassy area......
surrounded by trees......into this area a fairy appears
......she looks exactly as you have always imagined....with small and beautiful wings.

You approach the fairy......who is hovering
above the ground......You find you are not at all
surprised to see her there......she tells you that you
are special...not everyone can see fairies......She asks
if there is anything you would like and asks you to
make a wish......The answer pops into your mind
and you tell the fairy about your wish......and you
gently relax even more as you realize what you want
is attainable.

Snow

Breathe deeply and allow yourself to relax......and as
you do......you can imagine that you are walking
through a valley......towards the mountain......
which has snow at the top. As you get close to the
mountain......you find yourself walking uphill and
breathing in all the fresh air and the sweet smells
around you. As you get closer to the top you feel the
cold air, which is very refreshing. You find you are
making great progress......as you get nearer and
nearer......to the mountain top......your feet slip
slightly on the snow and the snow......which gets
deeper and thickens as you keep walking uphill......It
isn't difficult......you feel wonderful and you have
energy that you didn't know existed. When you reach
the top of the mountain......you see a cave that leads

you through a tunnel......the tunnel has a bright light......You find that as you follow this bright light......it leads you to an opening the light is escaping from......as you walk through, it uncovers a beautiful garden......with so many beautiful flowers......roses in pink......orange......and red......in fact so many colours......and so many other types of flowers......you smell the fragrance......it is so sweet and delightful......By the side of the garden you see a small stream with very clear water and beautiful fishes swimming, following the current of the water......As you walk by the stream you see two white swans......you wonder how they have got here......but you just accept it......you can't be bothered to question. It is so relaxing and pleasant to just accept that life has many miracles to offer......if you care to look for them. You ponder over the snow...... and the freshness it brings......knowing that you can just go down the mountain......and experience the warmth. It is your choice......it always has been......the difference is......now you know this to be so.

DEEPENER

The paragraph below makes for a very pleasant inclusion to place between the Induction and the Suggestion scripts. It is a powerful affirmation, helping to allay anxieties or fears that may be in the back of your mind.

In this deep, special sleep......your subconscious mind......for your protection, takes note of what is happening around you......so my suggestions...... which are all for your benefit......go directly to your subconscious mind. There they are accepted...... because these ideas are for your benefit......these thoughts become firmly fixed deep in your inner mind......embedded, so they remain with you...... long after you open your eyes......helping you to change those things you want to change......for your own sake.

SUGGESTION SCRIPTS

Suggestions are words in the form of instructions to encourage your inner mind to change to a more appropriate behaviour.

Pointers for Successful Suggestions

Each Suggestion script provided is carefully created to be a guide. You will be able to use the suggestion as it is, or introduce your own words to make it more tailor-made to your problem, or you can even select paragraphs from each as a type of mix-and-match. Whatever you decide, you can be sure that even if you should choose the 'wrong' Suggestion all that will happen is that your mind will edit out the unnecessary words and decide whether or not to activate the wanted ones. Minds are well protected for our inadequacies, so there is no need to worry whether you have it right or wrong.

As mentioned in Chapter 5, some people are visual and others are non-visual. If you are non-visual like myself, then you will probably find it more of a chore if a Suggestion is very descriptive. The suggestions included have been chosen to suit different kinds of readers. Some are short and crisp, others long and descriptive. I have also included some scripts developed from ideas from some of the people on my training courses who are now successful practitioners.

When dealing with the mind there are many variables and what works for one may not work for another, but should you choose after some practice to create your own suggestions, here are 8 useful rules to remember for formulating a powerful Suggestion:

1 Use the Present Tense
2 Be Positive
3 Be Specific
4 Be Detailed
5 Keep it Simple
6 Use Exciting, Imaginative Words
7 Be Realistic
8 Keep it Personal

Use the Present Tense

Always form ideas as an already accomplished fact, for example 'I am', 'I see.' In other words, always suggest that you are already acting out the behaviour change you desire. Say 'I am confident' or 'I have confidence,' for example. Direct suggestions for future behaviour must also be in the present tense:

'I always feel comfortable when …' 'Day by day I feel more enthusiastic about …' and 'I am more sure of myself.'

Be Positive
Eliminate every possible negative word. Don't mention what you are trying to change. Create a mental picture of what you want to move towards as if it has already happened: 'I am more confident,' not 'I will be more confident' or 'I would like to feel more confident.'

Be Specific
Confine your suggestions to one area; do not try to cover a collection of problems all at once. For example, do not tell yourself, 'I feel confident, I control my weight and I sleep soundly.' This could be counter-productive. It's like the lazy man and his load – he tries to carry far too much so that he won't have to make a return journey, and ends up dropping everything and making more work for himself. Try not to overload your subconscious with a selection of major problems.

Be Detailed
Analyse your goal and structure your Suggestion script to cover every detail of your desired changed behaviour or attitude. Don't just say you want to succeed – detail how and what goals you would like to reach.

Keep it Simple
Speak to the subconscious as if you were talking to a bright six-year-old. The subconscious may well be very sophisticated but there is less chance of confusion if you keep the wording

plain. The English language is full of words that have more than one meaning, so think carefully before you give your instructions to your subconscious.

Use Exciting, Imaginative Words

Make your suggestions full of feeling, excitement and quite graphic, powerful words, such as 'exciting', 'wonderful', 'dynamic'.

Be Realistic

There are circumstances where it is wrong to suggest perfection. For example, saying 'I am happy all the time' would not be a realistic Suggestion, and would probably be rejected by your subconscious. We all know there are times when we are not happy, when happiness would not be an appropriate response at all (for example at hearing of the death of a friend), so trying to programme your subconscious in this way will only fall flat.

Keep it Personal

Structure suggestions for the change you want to see in yourself, your attitudes and actions. You may not be happy with the behaviour of others, but the easiest way to initiate change in the people around you is to change yourself.

Picture yourself as you want to be. Your Suggestion should describe *action*, not ability, and suggest the exact improvement you wish to achieve.

A SIMPLE RELAXATION EXERCISE

You can tape the following suggestions by reading the words slowly into a tape recorder. Or you can read it first and then 'image' the process. You can use a favourite chosen Relaxation Induction (*see pages 74–94*) at the beginning to ensure a deeper relaxation. It is advisable first to read the chapter on how to hypnotize yourself (Chapter 5) before practising these exercises.

Your subconscious can be very positive and intelligent......things are linked......one to another...... think about the old rhyme......'The foot bone is connected to the ankle bone......connected to the shin bone......connected to the muscles......connected to the nerves......connected to the brain......' let yourself think upon the many inter-relationships......and interconnections......between mind and body...... body and behaviour......mind and behaviour...... now, review the significant traumatic events in your life......which could be related to your problem...... let this happen like a dream......which flashes through your mind......seemingly in an instant.

Consider how a child has a certain learning capacity......based upon immature thoughts...... and feelings......which are typical to children......as a person becomes an adult......it is possible to review these experiences......and re-interpret them from a more adult perspective......you need not consciously remember all the traumatic events......but your inner mind can reconsider the important ones from a more mature perspective......incorporating all the learning and understanding you have gained through the years......invite your inner mind to follow these guidelines......and then wait for your responses......when you have finished......allow yourself to come back......aroused from your daydream in a relaxed and calm state of mind......

[allow approximately 3 minutes of silence]

......allowing you to feel refreshed......and alert......and more free......now let your eyes open.

A BASIC RELAXATION EXERCISE

The Countdown

This type of exercise helps to control tension. Practise it once a day for three weeks. It gives you a chance to establish the habit of relaxing. Then practise it once a week for a short time. Later, a booster every now and again will suffice.

Close your eyes and take a deep breath in......allow yourself to exhale fully and completely......making sure to get the last air out of your lungs......breathe in again......as you inhale, allow yourself to see the number 1 in your mind's eye......at the same time focus your mind on your inhalation......hold your breath for approximately 3 seconds and then exhale ......as you breathe the air out fully and completely......mentally say to yourself '2' and visualize the number 2 in your mind's eye......breathe in again......and mentally visualize the number '3'......hold your breath for 3 seconds......and then exhale fully and completely......while mentally visualizing and saying '4'......inhale saying '5'......and exhale again saying '6'......always remembering to visualize the number and focus your mind on your breathing......inhale and say the number '7'......and exhale counting '8'......then '9'......and now '10'.

Repeat the full sequence once again, keeping your eyes closed.

Picture yourself resting comfortably. Visualize it in your mind's eye......you are so relaxed......

Count backwards from 10 to 1 easily and more quickly than you counted down. Open your eyes.

This simple exercise allows your body to recharge, even if you are doing it for only a few minutes. If you have any difficulty in visualizing the numbers, just practise clearing your mind regularly and be patient. Remember the old saying: 'Practice makes perfect.' It may be wise to remember that the more you try to relax, the more tense you can get. So don't try, just routinely follow the instructions.

The paragraph that follows can be added to any of the scripts in this book to encourage relaxation in your everyday life.

You now realize that relaxation is essential to your well-being and you also realize that it takes only a few minutes a day......You find that you look forward to your special time of relaxing. It may be just before you

sleep......just before you get out of bed in the morn-
ing......or at special times in the day or evening......

Whatever you choose......it becomes a natural
habit......easy......pleasant......a normal part of
your everyday life......and you find you feel so much
better day by day as you relax so naturally......

The rest of this chapter contains Suggestion scripts, organized as follows: scripts to help overcome different types of phobias; those to help with anxiety and anxiety-related problems; and those to combat panic attacks and rebuild your self-esteem and ability to cope with the difficulties of daily life.

Before each script, use one of the Inductions scripts above to ease you into hypnosis. Remember, too, to include on your tape the Counting Out script (*see page 71 in Chapter 5*). If you prefer, when taping the scripts for your own use you can substitute 'I' and 'me' for whenever 'you' and 'your' are used (for example, saying 'when I am outside I am calm......my heartbeat is steady and my breathing is regular' rather than the scripted 'when you are outside you are calm......your heart-beat is steady and your breathing is regular').

PHOBIAS

In the general rules for creating Suggestions, above, I mentioned not using negative words. This needs to be monitored with common sense. There is a discipline that believes that the inner mind does not accept negatives and disregards the word 'not' – for example that if you were to try to programme the ideas 'I never overeat' or 'I will not smoke,' the mind would eliminate the negative words, leaving you with the instruction 'I overeat' or 'I smoke.' This is not strictly true. For years I have had negative words in my 'stop smoking' script and I've been able to show a 95 per cent success rate. So you may find that there are a few negative words in some of the scripts below; their use is limited but they can be just as effective in the right context as more positive ones.

It may be prudent to note that the word 'will' may give the impression of the future and is, therefore, unwise to use. For example: 'You will feel free and at ease with the people around you.' The subconscious takes things very literally and, therefore, the mental programme may not be put into operation for 20 years or so.

As mentioned earlier, your success rate for using these self-help methods will depend on your commitment, the script you use and the seriousness with which it is executed, and whether your phobia is trauma-related phobia or not.

Agoraphobia – Fear of Going Out

The accepted meaning of the word agoraphobia is a fear of crowded places and open spaces, derived from the Greek words 'agora' meaning market place or place of assembly, and 'phobos' meaning flight or panic. But a more accurate description of agoraphobia is an exaggerated fearful reaction to being away from the safety of one's home.

Agoraphobia Script

Relax your body......let your body go limp......and comfortable......allow yourself the luxury of releasing all the tension......help yourself along by slowly ......and lavishly......taking in a deep breath...... now gently and slowly let that breath out......empty-ing your lungs completely......breathe in slowly once again and now let that breath out calmly and com-fortably......Once again, breathe in slowly and notice how you feel so much more relaxed......and you now begin to release that breath......see your body loosen-ing......floating through what is happening......that wonderful......pure......relaxation......allowing time to pass......and perfectly willing to let the time pass......detach yourself from any feelings and thoughts about what is happening......let your inner mind instruct your body that there is nothing at all physically wrong with you......all that has been hap-pening is that your over-sensitive nerves are playing tricks on you......and you are misreading them...... Just like sometimes excitement can be mistaken for fear......so many other feelings can be mistaken.

From now on......slowly and comfortably...... you will find you can venture out into the places which once made you nervous......you find that each day that passes you feel comfortable and more at ease......very relaxed and calm in these places...... You even feel pleasantly excited......and look forward to going out......the more you venture out the easier it becomes......and the calmer you become......your confidence grows and you feel so very proud of your achievements.

You can go outside your house whenever you want to......when you are outside you are calm, relaxed and in control......your heartbeat is steady and your breathing is regular......you are confident and happy outside in the fresh air......you picture yourself going to visit friends and enjoying their company.

Your home is a comfortable place to be......but you accept that you can go outside happily and confidently whenever you desire to do so......picture in your mind someone asking you if you are staying at home today and you say......'No, I am going out'......you say this proudly and mean it.

You no longer focus on people's attention......if people seem to look at you it just won't bother you at all......it will seem just as if they are observing you with some slight interest......it will not bother you in the least......you have no need to feel self-conscious because you are so calm and relaxed, and whenever you need to do something quickly you find that is easy too......You take pleasure in observing other people and life in general......Now you find all you need to do to relax......take a deep breath......and allow that relaxation to soothe your body......and mind...... allowing you to enjoy where you are......and deal with any obstacles that arise......Your mind clears and you find it easy to do all the simple things...... that were once so easy......and have become easier again......You take control of any situation easily

......whenever you need to......without a second thought......it comes so naturally......Very soon all the worries of the past will be in the past and your future is bright and at the pace you feel comfortable with.

Fear of Heights

As you relax deeper and deeper you find that the resources are within yourself to help yourself lose that old unwarranted fear of heights......Picture yourself climbing towards the top of a ladder......watch yourself shake with fear and see your fright......now allow yourself to see that the effects of fear can look very comical. Imagine a grown adult scared to death of a tiny spider, running away in a panic and squealing......Your fear is just as funny to a person who is not afraid of heights. You may have felt in the past that your fear is protective......but you know it to be destructive......now picture yourself in a real past situation when you were high up and it frightened you......imagine yourself reversing the process...... like running a video backwards to where you began before you were high up. Do this three times and then rerun a new picture of yourself climbing up with ease and without any discomfort......See yourself happy and enjoying the experience, knowing that your natural protection is always there......you have just erased the unnatural protection that has been causing you such distress in the past......no more......now life is much easier and your world is so much more safe. Practise again with your ladder now, noticing that you can get higher easily......without fear...... each time you practise in your imagination...... you realize there is no fear left......and this is now your reality.

Fear of Open Spaces

In a moment of total calm......you find yourself able to see your life more clearly than ever before......Like your perfect reflection in a calm mill pond......for the first time......you can really see yourself with clarity.

Nature makes everything special......unique ......and so that we can see things distinctly...... nature places a space around each of its gifts...... Without this space......life would be an endless blur of things......The bigger the space......the more we are being asked to appreciate that which we already have and also that which we are about to uncover.

Life is a procession of discoveries......Every new encounter that we make enriches our life......Wide-open spaces make it easier for nature to weave its own kind of magic and allow you to create a special space in your mind where you do not have to think......You can just be completely relaxed and take in with absolute wonder......how vast and all-encompassing your life experience has already been.

In your mind......you begin to tune in to nature ......As you begin to recognize something or someone, you now take the time to imagine some space around them......You now enjoy every moment that you spend with space as a treasure......from deep within the gifts of this space......will be made clear to you without the need to think.

Space is both a friend......and a magician......for it is always through a space that gifts appear.

Fear of Storms

As you sit here on this beautiful blue-green planet......it is worth remembering that nothing happens quite by accident......There is a good reason why the Earth is this beautiful......and that is because it is being constantly nurtured......and fashioned......by the forces of nature.

The forces of nature are so strong......that it is often all too easy to forget......that we too......are part of the forces of nature......Sometimes people can be like storms. Sometimes the forces of nature are so strong......that we wonder about our own safety......It is at times like these when you will remember that everything......and everyone......is exactly where they are supposed to be......for their highest possible learning......and growth.

It is even part of life's enriching experience ......to truly experience the fact......that because you are kept safe......it makes you stronger and also a lot wiser.

Nature has equipped you with all the gifts that you need to look after yourself......The most important of these is the ability to stay calm......The next is to consider your choices and this is why calm is so important. Now when you hear a storm approaching......the very fact that it is to keep our planet safe......and nourished......relaxes you and so you can enjoy the safety of the noises. If you are at home you make yourself safe and comfortable so you can enjoy the elements, knowing that you are safe and warm and comfortable. If you are outside then your mind instantly clears so you can find a safe haven quickly and easily, knowing your mind is your friend and it will create strategies to direct you to the safest place.

Choices are both created......and recognized within your imagination. For your imagination to be clear......you first find your inner calm......Effortlessly, creative solutions will offer themselves......and you can then pick the one that feels most appropriate.

Fear of Crowds and People

*Imagine you are speaking to one of your closest friends and feeling at ease with what you are saying......
As you are talking a few people start to enter the room......It is a large room and there is plenty of space......You realize that this room is fitted out for a meeting, with plenty of chairs and that the people coming in are preparing to settle down on the chairs for a talk......Because you feel so relaxed you realize that people strolling in are not bothering you at all......in fact, you feel more relaxed knowing that the people coming in are friendly......*

From now on you feel free......All the constrictions you have been aware of in the past disappear and you can enjoy the pleasures of being in the outside world free from fear......It is not a dangerous place and all unnecessary fears will disappear. You can imagine them being put down a waste chute...... thrown away in the rubbish bin or locked away in a trunk......or you can create a method yourself now......

[30-second pause]

......You find that this new strategy clears your mind so you are able to use your instincts to protect you from people or places that would cause you distress.

The freedom from fear will release you and enable you to enjoy places you go and people you meet......Your natural joy and sense of humour will replace your fears and you will automatically become more light-hearted and confident......This will attract people to you and you will make friends easily.

The following are Suggestions to get you back into meeting people after you have done some of the phobia work immediately above.

Because you no longer fear the unknown......the benefits to your social......domestic......and work life are limitless......You are happier each day because you enjoy meeting people and being in their company......and you enjoy and look forward to being in new places and situations......new places excite you.

With this newfound freedom you find that your personality is able to develop......exactly how you want it to be......You may want to be dynamic......you may want to be a good listener......you may want to be more up front......whatever you choose you find you attract and enjoy the company of the type of people you wish......who give you the friendship and companionship you are seeking.

You are happy in the knowledge that you have a more contented......exciting and dynamic lifestyle ......as you find it more and more easy to go out and socialize with friends of both sexes.

The world is a happy, friendly and safe place to enjoy......a place to meet people and to achieve fulfilment......a place to enjoy a newfound confidence in yourself.

As you enjoy the company of your friends...... they also enjoy your spontaneous and confident humour......You are realizing your full potential.

Becoming People Friendly

You have it in your person......all that you need...... is to make the change. Your subconscious now collects all your experiences......to give you the information......you need to be confident.

You find you are more easy in the presence of people......and act and feel more relaxed......Your comfortable attitude puts them at ease.

Your inner mind has all the information to create strategies to allow these changes......from books

......*TV......videos......people and the cine-ma......these have all been your guide......so your subconscious can gather the relevant information ......to allow your personality to develop as you wish it to be.*

No longer stunted by negativity......doubts and hurts......from the past......Now I want you to imagine a TV screen 1 metre high......and project yourself onto this screen......exactly how you don't want to be......Timid......unconfident......quiet......and reserved......See yourself as another person would ......Look at yourself on the screen......Now, on the top right-hand corner, project a picture of yourself exactly how you would like to be......you may want to use a role model......someone you look up to...... to help you design your new self......See yourself relaxed......and comfortable......with the people around you......even strangers......You exude a confidence with your easy manner......you don't have to be the life of the party to create this confidence around you......you can still be reserved and interesting.

Now switch the good picture in the right-hand corner across the screen......obliterating the old one......Notice there are dials at the bottom of the screen......These are emotional dials......if you adjust them you can adjust the picture......So start to improve the picture......build your confidence...... self-esteem......satisfaction of life......and all the positive emotions......which can now be easily adjusted......take a moment to do this......

[pause 30 seconds]
......*Notice how the doubts......worries......
and discomforts drain away......This is your blueprint to your subconscious......to allow your inner
mind to create the personality you want......Your life
is in your control now......and you can choose your
personality......by this simple visualization work
......Now just take a moment to enjoy the picture you
have created.*

The next few scripts deal with the common fears of animals,
spiders and snakes. For the animal one, you may want to
insert the name of the specific animal or animals you feel
phobic about.

Fear of Animals

*Imagine the animal standing behind the bars of a
cage......just like at the zoo......imagine this vivid-
ly......now say the word 'relax' in your mind......
breathe slowly and deeply......allowing your body
and mind to relax......Now the animal is closer......less than a metre away......Now you are the
animal......take the place of the animal......It is
calm and relaxed in your company and you are just
part of the scenery and it gets on with its life
......knowing that you are not a threat or harmful......and so it can relax and get on with its little
life......As the animal, create an image of how the
person ahead should behave......Now change places
back and bring with you the information from the*

animal......now observe the information......consider it and realize how clever and sophisticated your answer is......You feel so relaxed now......knowing that you are able to live in your world with the species that once frightened you......You know you take sensible precautions when dealing with any animal or insect......But you know now there is no need for any unwarranted feelings except calm......and happiness.

Fear of Spiders and Creepy Crawlies

It's because you want to live your life to the full......getting the most out of every day......followed by nights of blissful sleep......that it is now time for you to take charge of your life.

It is time to drop the irrational behaviour that no longer serves you......there is no longer the need to be concerned about insects......no need for sleepless nights, no need to look silly and helpless.

Spiders and other crawling insects have all got one thing in common......they're all cold-blooded......that means, to them, you may seem a positive furnace! Certainly, with spiders we make their 'hairs' stand on end in fear......in truth, they are very frightened of us and, not being aggressive, they run as fast as they can to get away from us......when we chase them. They are so scared that they roll themselves into a ball and play dead......hoping we will move out of their now terrorized life......if they can avoid you they will......your world and their world *exist side by side, but they want to have nothing to do with you......they just want to get on with their lives.*

We know so little about their world......and if we did......we wouldn't fear them......many insects do really useful jobs for us, like eating woodworm......always remember that to them......we may even look like gods......compared to them we are huge......immense beings......to be avoided at all costs.

There is no need to kill them......because they cannot harm you......recognize the real situation......instead of your unreal fear......just let them be......going about their simple lives......or if the situation requires it......put a glass over them......gently slide some paper under the glass......taking care not to harm your small, wondering friend......then you can carry him to a place outside......your lives are separate again, as, indeed, your worlds will always be.

Remember that......FEAR......stands for Fantasies Envisaged As Real......negative fantasies are the source of all fears......'being' in reality means that you cannot feel fear......you can only respond to a situation in an appropriate way.

You need never react in unnecessary phobic fear again......from now on you can respond as a conscious being......responsible......and completely in charge of the way you live your life......from now on, you choose your life......THIS IS FREEDOM...... and it feels great!.

Fear of Snakes

Picture a snake in your mind's eye......I want you to look closely and see the beautiful patterns on the snake's skin......see how many lovely colours form these patterns and how they run down the whole length of the snake......see how they run down the whole of its body......see how it moves......so gracefully through the grass......noble and serene.

Take time to see it clearly......enjoy these few moments watching this beautiful creature......take note of how very sensitive it is......see how alert it is......how it is ready to flee at the slightest movement or sound......see how it hugs the ground, almost too afraid to be seen......how timid it is......say to yourself that you will have only admiration for this elegant, timid, beautiful creature......that you will never be afraid now that you have come to admire and respect snakes.

Tell yourself how lucky you are to share moments like this with the snake......and if you have the pleasure of seeing more snakes......then you will be able to appreciate their beauty and elegance...... let yourself luxuriate in the feeling of being part of this whole beautiful creation......how privileged you are to be able to share it with such a fascinating and mysterious creature.

You have your natural instinct for keeping your distance when necessary......but you no longer have the fear that gets in the way of that natural instinct......your inner mind naturally protects you, while allowing you to come to terms with the beauty of life and its inhabitants.

In Chapter 2 we saw a list of some common and not-so-common phobias. Here are six Suggestions to combat phobias about the dark or the unknown (a form of claustrophobia), flying (a form of acrophobia), the number 13 (triskaideka-phobia), dirt (mysophobia), blood (haematophobia) and death (necrophobia).

Fear of the Dark and the Unknown

Now is a great and momentous time in your life......for you are about to undergo a really positive and healthy change......a change that is a big part......of your own evolution......mentally moving up......to a higher level......

From now on......you only think of the dark as a place......where there is an absence of light......You now realize......that thinking of white as good and black as evil is not only silly......but dangerous ......Even good and evil are just beliefs......for everyone sometimes makes mistakes......this does not make them evil......they simply lack illumination......Lacking illumination is not a crime......but it is where we find ourselves......when we allow ourselves to worry in the dark......

Even parts of our mind may seem hidden to us......you may even have worried about them...... no need......for they are easy to open up......as soon as you open them......the light rushes in......they are hidden because you or someone......have given it a name......'The Unknown'......

We all love mysteries......Writers and film-makers love to lead us on a journey......conning us into believing that there is......something......in the dark......They prey upon your imagination......and you get a thrill......you no longer need to believe in evil. From now on......you never allow yourself to take on......anybody else's fears or unhelpful beliefs ......No matter what their intention is......these would be the beliefs that enslave you.

Once you were scared......now you've learned how to deal......with the now......and what's real......Single-handed......you conquer......the bully in your mind......The one that survived......by making you blind to the fact that in truth......there is only one fear......that is of......fear itself......

Fear has gone......you can cheer......From now on you'll find......you are free to explore......The world is your oyster......and you are not poor......So hold your head high......Recapture your life......as you reach for the sky

Fear of Flying

You find that you can relax now whenever you would like to......when you are in a situation that before may have caused you anxiety when there was no need for it......you take a deep breath and a wave of relaxation flows through your body. As you feel so calm and relaxed, you imagine you are setting off for the airport......*you are surprised and happy to realize that you feel relaxed and comfortable about the journey......you imagine the trip to the airport......you arrive at the airport and check your baggage in and you feel so calm and relaxed......ready for the flight and looking forward to arriving at your destination......it is now time to go to the departure lounge......as you walk along, you casually look out of the windows and see the planes taking off and landing......some are parked ready to take on more passengers......you find the sight relaxing and as you take a deep breath, you find yourself even more calm and relaxed.*

The time goes very quickly as you await your boarding call......when it is announced you are looking forward to getting onto the plane and making yourself comfortable for the flight......you feel very comfortable and relaxed as you walk along the corridor to board the plane......you board the plane and find your seat......you feel very calm and relaxed as you watch the flight attendant giving you your instructions......the plane starts to taxi to the runway and you look out of the window and, as you do, a wonderful feeling of calm flows through you......as the plane revs its engines ready for take-off, you feel confident......the engine noises relax you even more......as the plane takes off and settles into flight, you feel a wave of relaxation flow through you...... and you realize you feel content and comfortable......you may decide to doze or read, have a

*conversation or even watch the in-flight film......
whatever your choice is, you find you are enjoying the
flight and you take advantage of the comforts offered.*

*The plane now begins to make its descent ready
to land and, as you take a deep breath, you relax and
enjoy the descent of the plane......the plane lands and
as you prepare to disembark, you feel refreshed and
enthusiastic......you look back on the flight and realize you have enjoyed the journey.*

Fear of the Number 13

*For some time now you have had a problem with the
number 13......and you may even have evidence that
the number 13......causes you problems......You
may know people......who are absolutely convinced
that the number 13 means trouble......As we all
know......this is called superstition......*

*Superstitions get out of hand when people ignore
facts......and let their imaginations run riot......The
basis for this superstition......is based on the little-
known study of numbers called Numerology......You
do not need to believe in it to understand......that it
is numerology that links Astrology to the Tarot......
Tarot is a set of cards that many people believe
in......using them to learn lessons about their lives
......Tarot readers claim......that big changes can
be foretold......by the 13 card......This card can
be either a warning......or the bringer of exciting
change......depending on where it appears within the
reading......*

But the reason that the number 13 Tarot card ......gets such a bad press......is because its name is 'Death'......In the context of a Tarot reading......this card means only 'change' or 'realignment'......Some people prefer to call it......the Prince of Change

It is also worth knowing......that the number 13......is revered in many parts of the world......as 'the bringer of change'......a force that is equally for good and bad......It tends to be good if you are good......but bad if you are bad......In Eastern terms......it is a form of karmic readjustment...... You get what you give......

In the Western world......the number 13 causes fear......because many religions declare us all to be sinners......The problem is not the number 13...... but the fact......that we allow ourselves to think that we are bad in the first place......

So the 13 is reputed to preside over change ......you only have to understand where the superstition comes from......If you live a caring life......sharing love......then the number 13 will either mean nothing to you......or it will be your friend......

Mysophobia – Fear of Dirt or Germs
Feeling comfortable as you are......and deeply relaxed......you understand that you are both safe and well......You are the living embodiment of several million years of evolution......It is amazing to think......that once upon a time......this planet had no life upon it at all......First came the plants under

water......then the atmosphere......and then much
later......came living creatures......

It may seem unusual to talk about the begin-
nings of in life this way......but we are descended
from out of this primordial soup......and everything......absolutely everything has an important
part to play......

The funniest thing of all......is that we often
think of ourselves as separate from the
planet......when nothing could be further from the
truth......the only thing......that separates us......
from any other living creature......is the way we're
put together......We are all made of the same
stuff......We are the living face of the planet......one
life-force in many forms......We are complicated
chemical factories......the human brain is far more
powerful than any computer......and we......like all
life......are evolving all the time......Because we
interact with all forms of life, both big and small
......we have behaviours and language......to deal
with the big creatures......and immune systems to
deal with the small ones......

Our immune systems work best......when constantly exposed to new mild strains of bacteria, virus-
es and germs......It helps us to build antibodies
......in the same way that vaccines work......The
Aztecs and Incas were not wiped out by the European
invaders......but by the diseases that they brought
with them......

There is much to be said......for the expression

......'What does not destroy me......makes me stronger'......so do not worry about colds and flu ......in the long run......they are actually good for you......

When it comes to food......you instinctively use your eyes and nose and taste......These senses combine to give us an amazing ability......to sense if food is good......the appearance, colour, texture, taste and above all smell......will guide you......you will be doing all that you need to do......your body is the marvel that does the rest......

Fear of Blood

In your deeply relaxed state......you are able to look at any subject......in a detached......and dispassionate way......as if you were seeing it on television......It is quite normal to find the sight of blood unpleasant......but it is not because blood itself is bad......but rather because we tend to associate blood......with pain......and maybe even death......

Some people fear hospitals......and yet hospitals are really where people go......to be cured......Blood is much the same......in that we see it......and think the worst......when in truth......even more than water......blood is the liquid of life......oxygenating, protecting and feeding our bodies......our bodies have the ability to make blood quite easily......so losing a bit is hardly a problem......Fresh blood ......like saliva and sweat......is not dirty......

From now on......you see blood differently ......You are still happier when it is inside someone's veins......but you are no longer worried by the sight of it......sooner or later......you may even want to take a course in first aid......because if ever someone near you is injured......a few simple actions could save this person's life......and all that it takes......is to stay calm and remember what you've been taught......At ease with the body and its fluids...... you too......one day......could be a life-saver......

Fear of Death

Now is as good a time as any......to take a good look at life......and what it is......that we actually live for......Very often our lives......seem to have little rea-son......After all......living is supposed to be fun......

The only thing that you can be sure of in life......is life......beyond that......everything is con-jecture......It is true that our bodies......at some stage......may no longer appear to have life in them......but is that really death?......We just have no way of really knowing......

Many people believe that you are not your body......that you......are where your consciousness is......that when your body is lifeless......you have gone on to live elsewhere......This doesn't have to be heaven......you could be born again......It wouldn't have to be here on Earth......science is indicating that the probability of parallel universes......is incredibly high......Who knows?

Living is like making love......if you become obsessed with your finale......you will not be enjoying......the whole point of being there. It really is time......to smell the roses......and do what you want to do......today.

Death is like tomorrow.......it never comes...... we live every moment......but only in the here and now......Now......is all we have......and now......is all there ever is......As you look after your nows ......your tomorrows will look after themselves...... The next time you catch yourself worrying......you will remember the Latin saying Carpe diem – 'Seize the day.'

Sometimes we can 'inherit' or 'learn' a fear or phobia from our parents or others who have a significant impact on our lives. Here is a script to overcome such learned behaviour.

Adopted or Inherited Fear Suggestion
In this wonderful state......of deep relaxation...... you have become more aware than ever before......of your desire......to be completely at ease with yourself......For a long time now......you have sensed that your life has been progressing......Progressing along a path of learning......a path of wisdom......a path of acceptance. Deep inside you......for a long time ......you have begun to realize that it is not only possible......but quite natural......to live in happiness.

You've looked at the happiest people around you......and you've noticed how they are so casual that they even look and feel like stars......You've noticed that in truth......they are no different from anybody else......except that they have learned to accept themselves......They have learned that they don't need any excuses because they know that their best is good enough......They are self-assured...... and don't appear to have any fears......These happy people are mirrors of your path......you have been drawn to their energies......because of a deeper resonance......deep down......you recognize that what they have......you have too......

In this place of relaxation......you know that you too can recognize......and fulfil your own greatness......and you know that now is time......the time ......for you to release yourself from your fears......

A wave of calm now slowly spreads throughout your whole body......energizing you and empowering you......for you have already passed so many tests ......many that you didn't even know were tests...... You are still here......and you are very much alive ......Much of your life you have had to put others first......and now it is your time......time to be free......time to be free from not only your own past ......but time to be free of all your family's past...... you are now entering a time......where you can accept all that is helpful from your family's past and its culture......only now you are free not to carry on the fears......

From now on......every time that you feel fear, you will know instantly......if it is a fear that you have learned from someone else......maybe someone you loved dearly......maybe something that you once overheard......or maybe a fear that got your attention when you were small......Either way you are now ready to let these fears go......they have served their purpose......they have helped to define you ......and you now have a better understanding of yourself......You have also learned to have more patience and compassion for others......in return, others now show you more patience and compassion......You have learned that being vulnerable has allowed you to grow......and above all your fears have lead you along the path of learning......learning about expectations......and learning about trust ......At last you can trust yourself......trusting yourself to look after yourself......without fear.

As you drop your fears......those around you drop theirs......Fear is just a belief......You are not your beliefs......you merely act in accordance with them......but you choose them......Now is the time ......to choose......the beliefs that help you......and to let go of those that no longer serve you......A positive belief is like an angel......as long as you don't force it upon someone else......but a negative belief is like a tyrant......preventing you and those you love ......from really enjoying this wonderful life...... In truth we don't even need beliefs......we can just be......

You do not need a tyrant in your life......you do not need to choose one at all......Beliefs cannot be proved to be true......if they could......they would be facts......Fear......especially adopted fear or inherited fear......is just a fake......but it is a fake that we took on......to become wise.

We become wise......as we realize that we are all perfect in our own right......only the unfortunate believe......otherwise.

Keep on Checking

'Boy Genius Kills Himself' was the headline in the daily paper the day after I included the script below in this manuscript. The story highlighted a rare brain syndrome which makes the sufferers clever beyond their years. It is called Asperger syndrome. The condition means that youngsters, while articulate, often give the impression of being 'absent-minded professor' types. They find it difficult to get on with children their own age and are likely to be bullied at school.

Approximately 207,500 people in Britain have the syndrome, 47,000 of them children. It affects brain development and is believed to be caused by brain damage at birth. It is not the same as other forms of autism, as the sufferers do not have any special learning needs and can be academically gifted. They have a problem communicating because they do not understand non-verbal signals and find it very difficult to judge other people's moods. They tend to take things too literally, so that a phrase such as 'She bit my head off' would confuse them. A side-effect is obsessional behaviour; sufferers can get angry and upset if their routine is changed. The boy's mother said: 'If he got 99 per cent marks in an exam it would be the other 1 per cent that would worry him. In the end it got too much.'

There are many students who are in this terrible dilemma, not having the actual condition but suffering similar symptoms. The awful and dangerous effects can drag a student into despair; if the condition is not attended to the student can fall into a depression that can lead ultimately to a nervous breakdown and, in some tragic cases, to suicide.

The student who wrote this Suggestion was one of 12 taking part in a psychology research project. I was teaching psychology students my advanced hypnotherapy course and at one stage I asked them to design their own Suggestion script. The student wrote this script to help him over his nightmare habit of constantly checking and re-checking his written course-work. It may be difficult for someone who does not have this problem to relate to it, but I have found it is quite a common phobia, and the Suggestion is one that is easy to adapt for treating other types of compulsive or obsessive behaviour.

Constant Checking

What a relief when everything is properly done!......
You have finished all the work......you are so relieved
now......nothing bothers you anymore......you have
no more need to worry......you have finished writing
so many letters to all of your friends with whom you
have lost contact for so long......You have finished all
the assignments and essays which have been a night-
mare for months......All are nicely typed/written
......well-edited......all prepared and just waiting to

pass up......You have finished writing all the articles you need to write......all the stories you have to write......so wonderful......your style of writing is so attractive......the stories and anecdotes are so interesting......very creative......

You know your friends will be looking forward to hearing from you......knowing you have taken the trouble to write and giving them a feeling of self-worth......You find you have finished your writing so easily and quickly that you wonder why you ever found it such a chore......The result of your writing is a wonderful achievement that satisfies you......You know you have written fast, accurately and interestingly......what are you waiting for......just send the correspondence out now......No need to check so many times......hand in all the assignments and essays you have done......Don't be confused......you have written well......you don't need to worry...... don't need to wait......go ahead......send them.

You are now relieved as you realize that if you keep checking you will just be making unnecessary changes......not making the piece better or worse, just different......you decide to trust your inner mind with what comes out the first time. No need for justifying how easy it is to express yourself.

You are now confident that everything is done right first time and you only need to just skim over the work to check for mistakes and not change the contents......There may be one or two small mistakes but this does not bother you......you just correct them......they in no way spoil the work you have done......it is futile to waste time in continually checking and changing......you are realizing...... what you can do with the extra valuable time you used to spend checking......you can read a novel......go for a walk......chat comfortably with friends without the constant worry of checking...... have a sound sleep......What a wonderful life without constantly checking......no more, now you can enjoy your work......You are now free from the doubts and fears and look forward to reading your own work with confidence.

A Phobia about Your Handwriting

Listen and learn......write and convey thoughts and ideas......These you know to be vital principles of communication......As you write any word...... sentence......or paragraph......you can write it concisely and legibly......with the utmost ease......and quickly......You know that this is worth while because......Time is not being wasted re-typing or copying unnecessarily......and the recipients......are appreciating the personal touch of this form of communication......a handwritten a letter is viewed as a mark of good manners on many occasions.

As you continue to practise writing with care ......you find that you can improve your speed...... and retain the legibility......you are proud to display this skill......and you are finding better uses for the time saved by yourself......and by others......who *may earlier have had difficulty in reading your efforts......You are receiving their appreciation...... in many ways and you are......pleasurably surprised by the results.*

Procrastination

This condition can become phobic and restrict the progress of the sufferer.

Procrastination is a hindrance in your develop-ment......It holds you back from achieving your goals and is a negative part of your personality.

    It is time to let go......let go of putting things off......put this destructive behaviour behind you ......You find you are able to tackle the jobs you would normally put off......if other things crop up, you choose to do the things that need to be done first......You no longer waste time finding reasons to avoid doing the things that need to be done......Your energy is conserved and used more productive-ly......You are happy and satisfied with your suc-cess......Procrastination is now something of your past......Your future is bright and you find that you have so much more time now that you no longer have to worry and make so many excuses to yourself and others.

SCRIPTS FOR ANXIETY-RELATED PROBLEMS

Anxiety

It is because you now wish to savour life to the full......taking advantage of all the opportunities that come your way......that you have now chosen to reclaim your life......allowing an old habit to drop ......into permanent retirement.

There have been times......when things just seemed to get out of hand......times when you didn't feel in control......and a bit of anxiety crept in......it happens to everyone......it's a very important lesson that we all have to learn......Sooner or later we all have to learn about focusing our energy......In our everyday lives we have tasks to overcome......some have obvious solutions......whilst others will require us to learn and grow......The greatest cause of anxiety is lack of familiarity......over time, all things become familiar......over time we become proficient ......as if we've done these things all our lives......

We distress ourselves when we worry that we or someone we care for......is not yet ready for a certain task......We needn't worry because in this life......we tend to learn as we go along......the proof of the pudding is in the eating......You are now in that wonderful place of self-acceptance......ready to go forward ......living without anxiety......Deep down you already know that worrying is a waste of your valuable energy......You are becoming more and more *aware that when you move your energy towards a solution......your energy either makes things simpler.......or more complicated......worrying always complicates things.*

In the future you will instantly become aware of when you are anxious......because you will find yourself remembering the old tune that goes...... 'What's the use in worrying, It never was worth while, So pack up your troubles in your old kit bag and smile, smile, smile.' Every time this happens your life will change......because important events are about to take place.

You are now aware that in every situation where you must choose between two options......that there is always a third option......which is to do nothing......Often things sort themselves out fine...... without us having to tinker with them......

You have also learned not to presume that there is a problem......where none exists. Virtually all of the world's greatest discoveries have resulted from accidents or unexpected outcomes......Learning to appreciate the gift of the unfamiliar is the very quality shared by those......most consider to be geniuses......Now that you can recognize the feeling of the unfamiliar approaching......you are better placed than most......to keep your eyes open for the potential opportunities about to blossom......What was once your biggest worry......is now a major key to your happiness and success......and life just gets better and better......

The following scripts deal with fears that can contribute to the anxieties and worries posed by everyday life. Some are practical in nature (combating fear of driving, for instance, and improving your tennis), some more profound (as fear of ageing, immediately below).

Fear of Ageing

It is because you wish to be happy......accepting yourself......that you want to age gracefully......Ageing gracefully......is an art form......and has little or nothing......to do with looks......

All your life you have known......that you can't judge a book by its cover......and you have found......that there are far more meaningful criteria......than looks......that make up a person's worth.

We live in a society......obsessed with sell-by dates......You have become aware of this......and those obsessed with beauty and youth spend absurd amounts of money......trying to be something ......that they are not......You have really begun to appreciate......that a person who is healthy and happy......is richer than any fool......who comforts themselves......displaying their status symbols and money......

You can now see that this state of affairs......is lead by the most deluded......paying others to bolster their vanity......unfortunately this quest......for the elixir of youth......prevents our society from ageing gracefully......

Sooner or later they will learn......putting their money to better use......but in the mean time...... you honour your body's needs......You eat a varied......healthy and exciting diet......and you maintain a lifestyle......that allows you to exercise regularly......and enjoy the company of good friends......You sleep well at night......and you pick your friends carefully......As you know......your worth is in your experience......in what you have learned......and what you can share......It's how you are......not what you pretend to be......and you know that every line on your face......has earned its place......

They say a face without lines......is the face of a fool......a facelift can't change......the person inside......and poor is the man......whose skin is his pride......

Fear of Driving

As you breathe in slowly you find this breath travelling all the way through your body......bringing a wave of relaxation......When you get into your car......opening the driver's side door......You feel so relaxed......all the fear is eased out of your body......leaving room for confidence......and happy thoughts......Your subconscious will now find constructive ways of dealing with your driving......you find it becomes very easy......now your fear has subsided and gone completely......you find that your mind is clear......as you take to the road.

Not all fear when driving is negative......you need a certain alertness in reserve to avoid accidents......now all your fear will be this type of positive fear......to be used only when necessary......the negative fear is channelled into this much more advantageous emotion.

Fear of Taking Your Driving Test

As you approach your test day you realize that you are looking forward to it......when you read your highway code it seems much more interesting and easy to understand......because you are no longer nervous you are able to understand and retain the information much more quickly and easily......you feel more confident than you have ever felt with your driving......and you are happy to demonstrate your skills. When you drive......before your test......you feel relaxed and confident......all the work you have done seems to fit into place and you now remember the instructions easily and comfortably......You do this because your mind is clear from negative fears and doubts about your ability......Not all the fear when driving is negative......we need a certain amount of positive stress to avoid accidents on the road......now all your unnecessary negative fear will be simply breathed out as you relax when you enter the car......this allows your mind to clear......the relaxation allows you to have that alertness for driving......while at the same time enjoying the freedom from fear......

You automatically check your mirror and turn around to check the road before you set off. You find it so easy to change gear correctly, without effort ......your mind is clear and it is so easy to concentrate on the road automatically without effort......You feel confident with your decisions......Whenever you need to reverse the car you find it so easy to judge the pavement or surroundings......As your confidence grows your driving seems so easy and comfortable......As you guide your car to go faster, at the correct driving speed......you feel comfortable......you know that your subconscious is taking responsibility......you note all that is going on......you are well-prepared......when you need to be. You find you are enjoying driving and your new skill. At the crossroads you realize that there is no need to keep checking......you look and when it is clear you proceed......You picture a car overtaking you in your imagination and you see how calm and controlled you are......When it's time to slow down you do this smoothly and confidently. You realize that you understand perfectly all the road signs you see......They all make perfect sense and this adds to your overall confidence......

You now see yourself being told you have passed your driving test and you see how delighted you are......you see yourself telling your friends and family......you know they are proud of you, and you are proud of yourself.

Fear of Learning New Things

Now that you are so deeply relaxed......so at ease with yourself that for the first time......you will be able to truly appreciate......the amazing qualities of your mind......no longer will you ever compare yourself to anybody else......because you know that it's a pointless game......it's like comparing apples with oranges......Your own uniqueness makes it important that you learn different things from other people......that's why the world is such a clever place......there are some things that you are interested in......that should you pursue them fully......you would be considered an expert......This area is a subject that you feel truly passionate about......it is an area that you wish something could be done about ......With your heart in it......it doesn't feel like work......and that's why you are able to learn so easily and quickly.

It is always worth remembering that the only insults that ever seem to hurt us......are the ones that at some level......we believe to be true......but the reason we allow ourselves to think that insults are real......is that they represent an opportunity to learn more about ourselves......We can then carry out an internal audit......and make adjustments......

You care about yourself and now it is time to see if......and what......adjustments need to be made......

If we didn't do this......we would all end up completely self-centred and uncaring......With evolution we are becoming more civilized......and most of our advancement has occurred through learning...... Learning is the same as adapting......creatures that can't adapt become extinct......Living things by definition are constantly changing......whilst things that always stay the same are dead......Since our minds are living things......they function best as they work to stay up to date with new inputs, ideas and concepts......an open mind is a healthy mind......The more it takes new information on board......the better it functions......and the happier you feel.

The most amazing fact about the mind is that it has no limits......There is no concept that it cannot grasp......and what we know now......may only be a tiny fraction of what our children's children may know......There is no subject too difficult to understand......providing that it is explained simply and in a logical way......and providing that someone is willing to learn.

From now on you find the willingness to learn......not for anyone else but for you......for the first time you can actually feel the thrill that you get......when your mind finds the link between different bits of information......You start to seek out links......almost by instinct......and when you have found a link......your newfound confidence enables you to have the courage......to set about trying to disprove it......this is scientific thinking......if no one can find a way to disprove your theory, then you really have got something new......This might be the entrance requirement to academia......or maybe the idea for a product......or maybe a scheme to help people......

Your life and those around you will never be the same......Your passion for your chosen subject will quite naturally uncover links......into other associated fields of knowledge......and before long you are becoming known for your broad-ranging understanding......In fact your ability and desire......to see things differently......makes you a fascinating companion......in any circle.

Anxiety about Visiting the Dentist

I used a similar Suggestion to this one for my fear when I needed to have a tooth out. I was given an injection in the roof of my mouth, but I didn't even flinch. It was obviously a painful area, and the dentist asked me if it had hurt. I just raised my eyebrows in response – I hadn't felt a thing. When I left I kept touching my mouth to check if the tooth had been removed. When the numbness wore off, I still felt no discomfort whatsoever. Am I now still scared of dentists? No, but I will always use a Suggestion first, just in case!

Picture yourself now......so very relaxed......you have practised relaxation so that you find it is easy to slip into a relaxed state......and to your surprise, when you think of the dentist you no longer feel anything but calm......knowing that you can just calm yourself whenever you feel the need to do so......

As you travel to the dentist you begin to feel the luxury of calm......floating over you......as you enter the surgery you do not mind waiting......you can easily use the time reading or daydreaming of pleasant memories......this is your special time......When you are called into the surgery to have the work done you feel very calm and relaxed......the sight of the instruments or room just serve to allow you to be calm and comfortable......knowing you are looking after your teeth......As the dentist starts to work on your teeth you relax even more......any work that the dentist does......brings no discomfort at all......you just notice the work and the sounds with idle curiosity......you allow yourself to relax even more and daydream about wonderful memories or wishes you would like to bestow on yourself......If the dentist talks to you......you respond easily and effortlessly......he or she may be surprised with your calmness......and may even say so......you just find the whole procedure easy and relaxing, knowing that the work is necessary and that you will be happy with the results.

Fear of Failure in Sport

A few examples are listed below in order to help you create your own for the sport or recreation of your choice. To build a useful Suggestion concerning the pursuit you are interested in, you will need to ask an instructor about the basics you'll need to know to be able to improve. It is of little use to give yourself a Suggestion such as 'I am good at swimming' without instructions about what precisely you will have to do in order to flourish.

Tennis Service

You prepare for the service with confidence......you know exactly what to do......as you step up to serve you feel fit and strong......wonderfully relaxed and confident......knowing this relaxation helps your mind to clear......you have maximum concentration for the serve......You feel perfectly balanced with full confidence in your body to take up the correct stance......You know your inner mind has mirrored the image and will be automatically instructing you how to serve with ease and total concentration ......You see with confidence the exact spot in the opposite court where the ball will be directed......

The racket is held firmly in your hand......it is an extension of your arm......You throw the ball in the air at exactly the right height......Your arm swings in a long, powerful arc......at precisely the right time, you hit the descending ball......The serve action is smooth and powerful and sends the ball skimming over the net to the spot aimed for......

With each serve you become more and more confident......You feel content and excited......You now picture yourself winning......you are excited and triumphant......

For the Golfer

Take a deep breath and let your mind and body relax......as you let your breath out allow your whole body to calm down......and relax even more ......Your body and mind is so deeply......so deeply ......relaxed. As you relax deeper and deeper......you realize that one of your strongest desires......is to play golf confidently......in any situation......and any weather conditions......on any golf course.

Your subconscious develops a strategy for achieving your desire by way of visualization......By visualizing what level of achievement you wish to reach......you can determine the skill level......and the handicap you are comfortable to play at.

Visualize now by using an imaginary 1-metre high TV screen in your mind's eye......project yourself onto the screen......see yourself as a skilled golfer......build this picture exactly how you would like it to be......take some of your limitations away......and see what you can achieve with a clear view......without old, unnecessary doubts......and negative thoughts about yourself......that you have believed to be true......when you know deep down......they are not.

This is a special TV screen......you can create and adjust the image with the dials at the bottom of the screen......These dials adjust the emotions...... You can add extra confidence and pride......You can change whatever other emotion you want......whenever you need to......You can programme any game

situation......weather condition......and golf course
......this is your reference......your rehearsal......
you can recall it at will any time you wish.

Each time you switch on this TV screen......
your subconscious will guide you with this technique......preparing your swing......down swing
......follow-through swing......putting and follow-
through putting......you can hit the ball accurately
and perfectly to the targets and into the holes.

You learn from watching the club pros......and
your own experience of playing golf......These techniques increase your concentration......judgement
......ability to read the green......your swing......
and your ability to putt the ball.

Your subconscious brings forward inspiration......confidence and a positive attitude......you
can play in any situation......weather condition
......on any course......Your mind is clear in selecting
the right clubs......targets......and swing......

The crowd......the bunkers......roughs......
trees......hazards......and noise do not bother you
at......in fact, they guide you in a positive way
towards relaxation as you decide your target......and
the strength of your swing.

Your self-confidence increases......every time
you play golf......You are capable of applying your
skills so well......your handicap is reduced to the level you are most comfortable playing at......Your ability to reduce your handicap......rapidly reinforces
your trust in yourself.

*As each day goes by......you learn to trust your abili-
ties......so that after each round......your self-confidence is reinforced as your handicap is reduced
......Your great ability is noticed by your peers
......This newfound strength......and determina-
tion......grow because you know you are achieving
your strongest desires.*

Golf – for the Beginner

*You find it easy to follow the instructions of your
instructor......Your mind and body work in harmony......Following and mimicking the swing......per-
fectly......easily......each time you play......You
watch your favourite golfer......and your subconscious
takes note of their stance......their swing......their
confidence......and their strategy......Allowing you to
record the information......ready for when you need
it......You picture yourself easily playing like a professional......It is so easy for you as you have the confidence and a clear mind to remember instructions.*

Fear of Dancing

*Picture yourself hearing the music and dancing with
a partner......When you hear the music your body is
relaxed and the tension flows out of it......You feel
alive and energized......the sense of rhythm pulsing
through you......This allows your feet to move in perfect synchronicity.*

*Your joints feel free......you can dance effort-
lessly......with balance and grace......You express*

yourself freely through movement......each and every new partner flows in harmony with you......creating a perfect team.

Any new steps and moves you wish to learn you learn easily and quickly......Your inner mind mimics the instructor and so you have no need for excessive practice......All the new information is stored in your subconscious and you have instant access to it......allowing you to perform new material spontaneously and without having to think about it.

Picture yourself performing and dancing with confidence......you enjoy it......You feel more energized and you move more freely......You love the ability to move in any way you please......capturing the rhythm of the music perfectly.

Towards Greater Self-expression

Imagine every step you have danced and put the best performance from every step into one super performance......Image in your mind's eye......a dance floor/stage......You will find you can easily see yourself dancing beautifully and naturally......You rehearse it in your mind......and as you do so you relax even more......You have a perfect sense of rhythm and you are completely immune to audiences......The noises from the people around you ......however busy and overpowering they may be ......don't bother you......in fact you relax even more with the sounds around you......you are full of energy......alert and so confident......you can do anything......You have the capacity......ability ......and motivation to dance your best steps ever, consistently.

 If you are to follow your partner then you find that it is so easy to read his/her body......you feel and sense their moves. It is so easy to be in step with them.

PANIC ATTACKS

This section deals not only with Suggestions for a panic attack but also contains scripts for coping with stress and difficult emotions, and enhancing feelings of self-worth and control in your life.

Here are a few self-hypnosis scripts to combat certain common triggers for generalized panic attacks.

As you go deeper into relaxation......you feel all the stresses......and strains......and fears......seeping away. It is as if there is a stream......with clear...... clean......water......washing away the unpleasant feelings and emotions that have been interrupting you through your life......All the unnecessary fear that has caused your restrictions......stopping you doing the things you would like to do......or simply causing you discomfort......all the negative thoughts that have prevented you from enjoying your life......are being swept away......visualize your whole body and mind being relieved of this debris......as it is swept out of your body and floats away on your breath as you slowly and gently exhale.

Imagine that you are building up your immune system and filling your stores of wellness as you inhale......until your system is glowing with energy and health......Your mind is extremely powerful and now you are instructing it to take care of you......erasing all the incorrect programmes...... that have plagued you for so long.

Imagine a wonderful glow beginning to fill your body, starting from your feet......this is your wellness glow......feel it moving you through your body as it cleanses, repairs and heals you......Feel how good your lower legs feel......and as the glow moves up your body......experience it healing as it flows through......experience your stomach......your back ......your arms and hands......feeling so comfortable as the healing glow travels at a languid pace through your body......monitoring and healing. Your head ......face......and scalp......feel so comfortable as the healing glow passes through......leaving your body comfortable and reinvigorated.

You know you now can access well-being through the power of your mind......this gives you a warm and comfortable feeling of confidence...... Imagine a television set......project an image of your-self on the screen......you are healthy and hap-py......This is your blueprint for your mind, so if it needs working on to produce a healthier picture you can work on it now......You will notice there are dials on the television set......these dials are emotional dials that you can adjust to produce the picture you desire. There is a dial for good health. Look where the dial is showing......and then adjust it to excellent health......when you have the picture that you are happy with......just allow the picture, and television, to fade away knowing that your blueprint for your inner mind is in place......you have set the programme into action......as you drift into deep relaxation you tell yourself that you are getting better ......and better......day by day.

For Panic at the Prospect of Having to Speak in Public

Imagine yourself arriving at the venue you are going to speak at......you begin to feel more relaxed...... It surprises you how very relaxed you begin to feel......In fact as you begin to see the people that you are going to talk to, you feel very comfortable and confident......your nerves become stronger and steadier......as your confidence begins to grow ......you realize that talking to a crowd is only like talking to your friends......your friends don't always agree with you and you have to find interesting ways to sway their opinions......in fact you find it interesting to sway their opinions......just as you will when you speak to a crowd......you have all the skills you need to communicate naturally......and you find that as you realize this simple point......you become less and less conscious of yourself......and less preoccupied with yourself......you find that you are looking forward to speaking to a group......

in fact any group......after all, they are all people like yourself.

You imagine yourself at the end of the talk ......or speech......and you are delighted to see the audience applauding......and happy......and smiling......You can tell they have enjoyed your talk and felt easy with your confidence......and easy manner......you were able to put your points across easily. Work on your picture, your dress rehearsal......until you are satisfied with the outcome......These are your instructions to your inner mind and your inner mind will find strategies to bring them into reality.

Visiting the Doctor's Surgery

As you walk into the doctor's waiting room you are surprised at how relaxed you feel......everything in the room only serves to relax you......You find you can relax easily......and if you have to wait you find it is easy to occupy yourself until it is time to be seen......When you are called to see the doctor...... you feel contented that you are going to be attended to by an expert and this confidence relaxes you. Your breathing is regular and comfortable as you walk into the surgery. You smile at the doctor and explain why you are there, knowing that the doctor is there to attend to you and give you an expert's opinion. You find you can sensibly take the advice given and ask the questions that you need to in order to understand......You feel comfortable and confident...... and you know that your mind is clear......and

sharp......while you are talking over your problem.
You realize that the doctor is a person......with
knowledge of helping people......You are able to use
his or her knowledge to find out what needs to be done
to create wellness......You also know that with the
right attitude in your mind your body can be instruct-
ed and helped while taking advantage of the wonderful medicines available to you. As you talk to the
doctor you realize that you can easily find out the
information you need......with a smile......and a
friendly and comfortable approach.

Body Awareness

You know you have many excellent qualities......you
are intelligent......kind......list your good qualities
to yourself......

In a moment I want you to count from 1 to 10
very slowly......after each number say 'deeper
and deeper'......when you have said this one of your
good qualities will pop into your mind......take a
moment to think about this good quality as you relax
even more:

1......deeper and deeper......
[allow about 5 seconds as you think of one of
your good qualities]

2, deeper and deeper......
[5 seconds]

3, deeper and deeper......
[5 seconds]

4, deeper and deeper......

[5 seconds]

5, deeper and deeper......

[5 seconds]

6, deeper and deeper......

[5 seconds]

7, deeper and deeper......

[5 seconds]

8, deeper and deeper......

[5 seconds]

9, deeper and deeper......

[5 seconds]

10, deeper and deeper......

[5 seconds]

As you mull over each of these qualities you realize that from now on you are far more aware and proud of your many good qualities......your confidence and self-acceptance will rapidly increase day by day......As each day passes you become more competent and successful as you improve your performance......leaving behind the notion of being a perfectionist......you find you accept failures and setbacks, as a nuisance......not as a disaster......more and more you find that you are a worthwhile person yourself......you find you can think more clearly, sort out your priorities, and enjoy your life.

You realize that your body is an ingenious part of nature......and that you are lucky to have a beautiful body......you know that if you have treated it badly that this will show......but this can be put right by eating correctly and exercising......You may have thought your body was not perfect in the past......but you also know that there is no such thing as perfection......the mind is such that if you allow yourself to focus on yourself too much it will pick at the little faults in your body......focusing on them so they stand out only to you......no more do you need to preoccupy yourself with worrying about your body......because you can look at yourself with a more sensible......and clear......approach......and see your body for what it really is......a beautiful piece of art that you can be proud of.

Panic Attack

This is a very good time to take stock......a time to truly seize the opportunity to help yourself......a time to be thankful for just how good life has been...... For in those times where we think we've given up hope......things still work out fine for us......at the time we feel crushed by self-doubt......all that......is now in the past.

It is now in the past......because that was how it was meant to be......For our highest possible learning......times of doubt......present to us the best possible way to learn the value......of making calm decisions......Now you understand that time is on your side......not against you......and you have learned that by speaking up early you can prevent problems later on......From a place of calm......

You don't speak up because you have something to prove......you speak up because what you have to say is important......it is important because you have considered your message and you do not wish to devalue the importance of your words......

You have finally learned to assert yourself...... because you know that your opinion is as valid as anybody else's. You have now learned that people are convinced by your honest, logical and calm manner and words......They are more than happy to discuss your views......The panic that you have felt in the past has acted as your teacher......it has taught you to observe......and more importantly, it has shown you......how easy it is......to be one of the sheep......

No more......No more and never again will you be a sheep......You once felt panic because you felt powerless......now you know that because you are now taking more time to notice everything......taking time in a calm and even playful way......that you are able to express your feelings and thoughts quite clearly......Every day you are able to use fewer words to say what you want......every day you are becoming more eloquent......and as a reward this makes you appear......even more attractive.

The greatest gift anyone can learn from panic......is clarity......this gift is now yours......and it rings out like the shepherd's bell......

Stress

I want you to picture yourself emptying your mind of all the unpleasant......memories......and feelings......and worries you have......I want you to discard them......throw them into a container......seal it up......and have it taken away......Now you have a chance to start anew with your life......with control......no unpleasant thoughts that corrupt your thinking......You now have control of your life and you have choices......Experience how it feels......how good it feels......Any new problems that arise...... you find easy to deal with. Instead of problems you think of them as challenges and let your inner mind find solutions that are easy and comfortable. You don't even have to work at it......Your inner mind does it for you while you are getting on with your life.

Picture yourself emptying your mind of all the unpleasant thoughts, memories and feelings you have collected through the years......you can do this by imagining you are using a gigantic suction vacuum cleaner......sucking all the negative thoughts out of your mind......there is now plenty of space to fill up with wonderful thoughts......This is easy......all you do is instruct your subconscious to do a search in your mind for all the positive and constructive thoughts that will be useful to you......The mind is so sophisticated it can do this in a split second......Now use your imagination and pretend that you have only nice thoughts......let your imagination start to roll. Imagine your life......your future with just a positive outlook. Picture yourself with this positive attitude ......and now look at what your imagination has come up with......explore this wonderful area...... Your inner mind will be able to show you the way forward......take a moment to allow your imagination to picture your future filled with positivism and pleasure......

[take a minute's pause]

......Whenever you wish to look at your life more clearly you can use this technique to allow your mind to advise you......Remember your inner mind has all the answers to your problems. It has the information to give you the best advice......take advantage of this facility......take some time out of your day to build your plan......Your inner mind will be there at any time to help you.

Mental Stress

You have decided to monitor your body's progress ......taking into account that as we mature and get older......our bodies need less sleep.

To help this process, any excess thoughts that cause inward stress......even though you are not aware of this inner action......your inner mind now allows you to sort it out on a conscious level so as not to create inner anxieties......All you are aware of is a conscious instinct that things need to be thought about......so they can be settled......your inner mind and body are no longer in the turmoil that creates stress......You notice you are able to relax more

......*your back and neck release......It may be every day or once a week or every now and then......you will know......your body will give you a sign by reminding you to relax...... You are able to do this by taking a few moments to relax whenever you feel it is necessary......No more ignoring your body signs ......you respect yourself and you operate with more mental efficiency......The result is an even more enjoyable lifestyle.*

Ego Script: A Filler to Help You Relax

As you relax......more and more deeply......your own self-healing forces are switched on......Muscles......Nerves......the very fibres of your being, rest and relax......Every system slows down......So your whole being rests......Healing forces check every part of you......Repairing......replacing and re-energizing......Soothing your mind and nerves.

So......this relaxation enables you to feel fitter and stronger in every way......Your nerves stronger and steadier......Your mind serene and tranquil ......you experience peace of mind......and a deep sense of well-being......as you drift deeper and deeper.

These feelings stay with you long after you open your eyes...... You feel more self-confident...... Your will-power......determination and self-assurance grow and develop...... You feel more comfortable......within yourself and within your surroundings......Day by day these positive feelings develop inside you......Day by day......life becomes more enjoyable......more fulfilling......You feel so much better......within yourself......and about yourself in every way.

The way your subconscious now protects you ......is to allow you to be more relaxed......and calm......and easy......and comfortable.

You discover......because you feel so comfortable......that you enjoy life much more......Your reactions are mature and natural......These changes occur because your subconscious mind wishes to take care of you as well as possible......Your subconscious recognizes your need to feel secure......and to be able to look ahead with confidence and optimism.

Whenever you relax into self-hypnosis you find yourself sitting on your garden bench in your garden......even more relaxed than you are now. In a few moments you can count back from 10 to 1...... and on the count of one......your eyes open......and you feel relaxed......refreshed......and rested...... and these feelings remain with you long after you open your eyes.

Grief Fear: Not Being Able to Get Over the Death of a Loved One

You know you have guts......and you know deep down in your inner mind that......[name of person who has died]......would be distressed to see you suffer at all......just as you would be upset to think of [him/her] suffering if you had died first......You are alive and healthy just the way that......[name]

......*would want you to be......you have a responsi-bility to life to keep yourself fit and strong and positive.*

You know you can easily escape for a short time with drinking or taking pills......but you have the guts and don't need to take that road to failure.

You have a wonderful, exciting personality and your experiences have given you an amazing amount of confidence. At the moment your confidence is in the shadows......bring it forward to where it belongs ......in the front of your life......Imagine your confi-dence being hidden by a veil......now find interesting ways to remove that veil to allow your confidence to surface once again......and rejoice in the freedom from grief. Grief can take over if you let it......there comes a time when it becomes self-indulgence...... and then it is time to move on......and let your loved one rest in peace.

Fear of Anger

Because you want to have a full and happy life ......you have good and positive feelings towards oth-ers......You realize that everyone has their own strengths and weaknesses......You tolerate and accept people as they are......without judging or analysing their actions and words......You learn to accept and appreciate these differences......You forgive others for actions or words that you disapprove of......You develop your sense of humour easily......and you no longer have to take life so seriously......You control all your hostile feelings......you feel only love and kindness towards everyone......you no longer expect people to behave the way you think is appropriate. You channel all your negative feelings into constructive ones......Your actions allow people to feel happy and good about themselves.

Confidence Booster

Because you want to become a confident person ......just conjure up an image of the word 'confidence' in your subconscious mind......see a cinema screen ......you are looking at yourself on the screen and you are directing yourself in a film......You instruct yourself to act with confidence......now look to see what image and storyline come onto the screen......because you are the director, you can adjust the film to suit you.

You give instructions to the actor, who is you, to look full of confidence......Every word you say is full of confidence......every step you make......is full of confidence......Your every touch......is full of confidence......you smile full of confidence......now watch the screen and watch yourself in the role of the confident person......

[60-second pause]

......Now your subconscious has the instructions it needs for you to be that confident person......you find that you see the changes......take a deep breath in......as you breathe out......breathe out all the insecurities and doubts......and fill up

with confidence......breathe in that wonderful confidence......day by day you will notice subtle changes that give you great pleasure as the confident person you are.

Greater Assertiveness

You know the key to success and enjoyment in your life is assertiveness......Because you want to be assertive, you are not afraid to ask for help when you need help......You are not worried about offering a constructive criticism to your colleagues and friends ......You can refuse to do a favour for your friends and relatives if you do not wish to do so......When your boss or someone else shouts at you or is rude to you......you can tell them that you resent their behaviour.

You feel good about yourself for asserting your rights......You know you have the right to change your mind. Others will respect you because you are honest with them about your feelings......and you treat them with respect......You know that the world is not perfect......but others will be more likely to change if you change yourself......you find you like yourself......and feel good about yourself.

It is such a relief not having to put on a mask and to suffer in silence......It is such a relief not having to pretend and lie......It feels so good to be able to be just yourself.

Because you can just be yourself you enjoy your relationships more......The barriers between yourself and others are removed......You really get to know others and others get to know you as you are......You feel a bond with other people and the world.

Fear of Not Achieving in Your Work

Your subconscious mind has the power to allow you to achieve exactly what you want......and you are now instructing it to prepare you to become an achiever......both in long- and short-term goals...... You are successful and your subconscious works positively for you......and you are full of confidence and have the knowledge that you have a wonderful inner mind......which helps you to achieve all that you desire.

You take pride in your professional appearance and you speak well and intelligently......with full knowledge of your subject......which you enjoy.

You now live your life and complete your work in a calm......relaxed......professional manner...... and cope very well in any emergency......or crisis which may develop.

Seven

CHANGE YOUR LIFE
WHILE YOU SLEEP

A nother avenue to explore that is so simple and quick it seems impossible that it would work.

❖ ❖ ❖

Sleep hypnosis enables the subject to direct the inner mind to do the work even before the conscious is active.

The specialist hypnotherapist has been likened to a computer expert who shows you how to work your computer and software. 'Hypno Sleep' can be likened to going to the computer designer for advice on creating your own programme. Your specially devised hypnotic Suggestion, even by passing the subconscious, helps you to make the necessary adjustments to ensure the smooth running of the equipment.

The way it works is that you create Suggestions to point out problems and ask them to be attended to. A Suggestion dealing with a specific phobia, for example, might read like this:

Mary has been creating stress and tension that is using up valuable energy while she reacts to the fear of......[her particular phobia]......Mary is ready for change and from now on she no longer needs to react in such a stressful way......she finds that she is able to be calm......and comfortable......and confident......in any situation that before caused her to have unnecessary fear......this new attitude enables her to see the situation as it really is......she now realizes that she no longer needs the fear......and that her inner mind no longer needs to use this inappropriate programme......any longer.

Until now, it has been generally accepted that trauma-related problems need regression therapy, but research in the last few years has proven that sleep hypnosis works for even these types of problems. It is not generally known in the UK and was developed by Jack Mason in the US.

After my book *Slim While You Sleep* (Blake Publishing) was published, many readers would write to me telling me it had worked for them and some asked me to do Suggestions for other problems of their own or for their relations or spouses. In my own case it was 100 per cent successful – it enabled me to get over my father's death without rehashing all the traumas I knew were directly involved, since the same traumas were the cause of a serious memory loss, a memory loss that I experienced for six years. The previous therapy work I had done to retrieve my memory was in itself traumatic, and I was loathe to have to go through the same, or similar, tactics to get rid of the anger and frustration I was feeling after my father died.

Even though I was suffering and knew I needed to have some treatment, I took six months needed to find this new therapy. When it worked for me, I knew I had hold of a very exciting method, more powerful than I could have imagined, and I was sure it could be adapted in some way for self-help.

With the advice and help of Jack Mason, I carefully designed and adapted the idea, at the time specifically for the person who wanted to lose weight but who didn't want to have to relive possible underlying, unpleasant feelings and memories associated with being overweight. Not, I must add, that any unpleasant memories which I have unearthed – in either myself, or in the thousands of clients I have helped in hypnotic regression – have ever caused any regrets about the therapy. In fact, they have led only to positive feelings. But there are many people who refuse to have therapy because of this fear.

Until the knowledge gained from this new technology I would have recommended that the only option after self-hypnosis for a troubling problem would be to see an advanced hypnotherapist; now there is another route. It is not foolproof, nor 100 per cent guaranteed – no treatment ever is – the likelihood of success depends on your own commitment. It really is up to you.

We live in a society that seems to take away all individual responsibility for fixing ourselves. This is your chance to take back responsibility for your own self-development.

THE CONCEPT OF SLEEP HYPNOSIS

Therapy work in hypnosis has generally been done while the client or subject is in an altered state of awareness, a type of daydream, but nevertheless, awake. When you are in hypnosis, you are always aware of what is going on around you. If you are asleep, you are not in hypnosis.

Suggestion hypnosis is just a specially adapted set of words, introduced while the subject is in hypnosis, that create a new programme for the subconscious part of the mind to follow. This programme brings about a change in the subject, resulting in more favourable behaviour. However, things may be more complicated if there has been a trauma-related incident directly responsible for and causing the unwanted behaviour. This trauma will either be forgotten or edited out by the subconscious and, therefore, prevent the conscious part of the mind being able to sort out the problem.

The following is an example of the Suggestion used in Hypno Sleep. It can break through and make changes disregarding even the most horrific traumas. It is carefully prepared for anyone with unwarranted fear problems and is all that you need to instruct your inner mind to repair possible buried traumas and prepare for new, desirable changes. The first few words are very important and need to be repeated. While asleep, this short instruction puts your sleeping mind into 'receptive mode': 'You can hear me but you won't wake up.' These all-important words set your inner mind to receive in this special state – not asleep, not awake, not even in formal hypnosis, somewhere else – a different depth, like a new wave band.

Because the Suggestions in sleep therapy are so much more concentrated than the Suggestions used in hypnosis, and you are addressing the higher self rather than the subconscious, I would recommend that you take professional advice if you want to create your own. You can contact my training centre for information (*see Useful Addresses chapter*) for a list of Hypno Sleep suggestions. They are a little different from the usual ones.

The Suggestion below is excellent for general fear attacks. All the words used are soothing and safe. It is not a good idea to fill the Suggestion with negative words. It is supposed to be a massage of the mind – and a gentle massage at that, not a punishing one.

INSTRUCTIONS AND DIRECTIONS FOR THE HYPNO SLEEP METHOD

First you will need to use a tape recorder to tape the words. An almost-loud whisper is ideal.

There are certain things that need to be said while you are sleeping to allow your inner mind to be able to accept the specially prepared Suggestion(s) without disturbing your sleep.

The words 'You can hear me but you won't wake up' need to be repeated several times. Then there follows the Suggestion. Begin in the same tone of voice: 'And now to sleep...' Repeat this twice to allow your brain to monitor the sound. Make sure the sound level is just loud enough for you to hear but not loud enough to disturb you. Then leave the tape blank until just near the end. This space enables you to go to sleep, so I would suggest getting a long-playing tape, for example, 90 minutes. If you find you take longer to drop off to sleep, then you should buy a timer and time your tape to come on at, say, 4 a.m. If the tape disturbs you, then you know you have it too loud for it to work, although it may also be that you have been brought into a state of half-sleep by your inner mind.

Jack Mason used to use this technique in hospitals when he would work with the terminally ill. He achieved astounding results in improving their quality of life.

Suggestion for Fear Attacks Created for Sleep Hypnosis

Use the spaces to break your sentence up:

> *You can hear me......but you won't wake up......you can hear me......but you won't wake up......you can hear me but you won't wake up......you can hear me but you won't wake up......And now to sleep......*
>
> *[let the tape run until there is only just enough time left to record what follows]*
>
> *Your inner mind is now being retrained for a new and beneficial programme......one of healthy living......and freedom from fear......the unwarranted fear you have been experiencing for so long ......Your mind is now programmed for harmony......your mind instructs your body cells to work towards health, and that leaves no room for unnecessary stress caused by the extra negative fear......This programme starts to release and solve trauma-related problems......that have been obstructing you up until now......Day by day you feel......look......and act*

*more healthy and in harmony with your life as you
want it to be.*

*You find that when......as before......you would
tense and become fearful......you now feel calm......
and clear-minded......You always feel in full control
of your emotions......and enjoy the confidence......
which has previously eluded you......No more......
you can now look forward to a wonderful life......as
your unresolved traumas are being attended to
......while you are able to get on with your life......
your inner mind working for you......with you......If
ever you feel curious and look for the negative
fear......you find you relax even more......your body
is calm and comfortable......and you feel comfortable
and at peace with yourself.*

*Whenever you use your Hypno Sleep suggestion
while you are sleeping......your inner mind allows
you to sleep while the important changes are carried
out......changes in attitude to begin to bring back
that natural self-discipline......and common sense
which helps you to be free from fear......Any fear that
is necessary for your survival and well-being will be in
excellent working order......but we are talking about
the extra negative fear that is in the way of you enjoying a happy and healthy life.*

Sleep hypnosis is just another tool you can add to your box of
mind-tricks. It is a safe and comfortable way to start to work
on yourself. The method needs practice and commitment, but
the positive benefits repay the discipline needed handsomely.

Eight

CASE HISTORIES

T his chapter concentrates on case histories where the cause of a phobia has been found by the use of regression therapy. The purpose is to show you where fear attacks can stem from, therefore widening your scope when it comes to helping yourself with your own anxiety, phobia or panic attacks.

Fear of Rodents

Sylvia had just taken one of my advanced hypnotherapy courses and was successfully practising hypnotherapy. She asked if I would help her to clear up a phobia that had irritated her all her life. She had dealt with her more major problems on a previous course and was now ready to tackle minor irritations, as she explained it. This particular minor irritation had caused her an amazing amount of worry and fear, which she had grown to accept.

She had a fear of mice and guinea pigs. She had allowed her children to keep them when they were little, but insisted they keep them safely in the shed. 'Their cages were so elaborately locked it was like Fort Knox,' she said. She explained that her fear that these little furry animals would escape was so severe that she'd spent many sleepless nights terrified about the prospect. She didn't even like to be near her children when they held them. Now she had grandchildren and they would tease her mercilessly, so she was suffering once again.

She pointed to a straw animal ornament that I had. She said that throughout the last course she had tried not to look at it. It reminded her of a guinea pig and she found this simple shape had created a horrible reaction. She cringed as she walked past it, not mentioning her irrational fear to the class. She had tried to ignore the ornament and protect herself from too much discomfort by sitting in a position that prevented her having to look at it.

I was grateful for this little representation of her fear. I knew that I could test the therapy immediately she came out of hypnosis by seeing if her reaction had altered.

She said her mother had been terrified of mice and would always stand on a chair if there was a mouse around.

In hypnosis I regressed her to the time that she had first had the fear. She was in the sitting room with her mother. She was about 4 years old. A mouse ran into the room. Her mother screamed and ran out, leaving Sylvia in the room with the mouse. Instead of coming back with a shovel to crush the mouse, as she normally did, Sylvia's mother went to a neighbour's house and stayed there for some time. Little Sylvia felt as if her mother had abandoned her, and she felt very inadequate. This inadequacy stayed with her all of her life. She constantly tried to over-compensate by looking after people and not putting herself first, always catering to others. She had become a drudge and now her children were grown up she wanted to enter into her own profession, but she had found it difficult to break the habit of always looking after everyone, constantly cooking for and mothering them.

When she was brought out of hypnosis I asked her how she felt about the straw-shaped animal that had previously upset her so much. She laughed and said her fear was gone and she couldn't imagine how such small furry animals could upset her so. She was amazed how that one experience with her mother had affected all of her life, adding to her low self-esteem which she was only now rebuilding.

The change in Sylvia was quite extraordinary over the next few days. She became strong and fully confident about her own opinions, and her work improved remarkably – she now had that previously elusive self-assurance.

A Letter from Sylvia Reporting Her Progress

How it was for me:

I had described my fear, or rather my terror, of mice, hamsters and rats to a group of students when I was learning hypnosis at one of Valerie's training courses. So up I stood and walked over to the chair in the centre of the room, where live therapy is demonstrated. Valerie said 'Let's stop that fear of small creatures for good, the feeling that Sylvia has of being tormented by her grand-children, and let's get rid of those primal screams.' I had just finished telling the class that I would let out a primal scream if ever I allowed myself, by accident, to be near one of the offending animals. What was more disturbing was that I felt repelled by the thought of these creatures crawling all over the children, in their hair, up their sleeves … horrible … it never occurred to me that it was a pleasant and happy experience for them. I felt revolted and was beginning to feel the same way about the grandchildren.

Under hypnosis I was taken back to a time when I was about 4 years old when I saw a mouse behind the sofa. My mother, who was also terrified of mice, rushed off to get a shovel to kill it. But she didn't come back. Instead, she stayed away and chatted to the neighbour. I was left with the mouse. I felt totally rejected and as if I was of no importance. Valerie pointed out how the little creature was in fact quite terrified itself, afraid for its life, in fact. This would not have been acceptable if I was in normal consciousness, I would not have been able to relate to the mouse at all, but in hypnosis I felt sorry for the little creature. We stayed in the memory, having the advantage of seeing the mouse as it really was, and visualizing how I could enjoy being with my grandchildren again and not appearing a complete idiot in front of them.

I came out of hypnosis and looked towards the straw ornament. I had been frightened of the sight of it on the previous course, and I was so used to these feelings that I had just accepted them, never even thought of mentioning them. I even sat in a chair facing a different direction, so I wouldn't have to inadvertently see the offending sight. I was able to test the therapy as soon as I opened my eyes. When I now looked at the object that had earlier frightened me, it didn't bother me at all. I felt very free immediately after the therapy, already viewing the world differently.

What is so very surprising since is that the grandchildren have not shown me any of their little creatures. I have not mentioned my cure to their parents or themselves, so no one but me knows how I feel now. It seems as if I was attracting the situation to myself by visualizing and expecting it to happen. The mice and hamsters no longer exist as a threat to me. I have changed my attitude towards them.

It's been three weeks and though I have seen my family most days I haven't come into contact with their pets. In fact, I even went to the shed to check out whether the mice and hamsters were housed there. They were, and I went into the shed but felt no fear. Now I am waiting to be tormented by the grandchildren so I can surprise them, but maybe I never will never get that chance.

I have just heard from Sylvia and she reports that not only has her phobia of mice and guinea pigs gone completely but also her fear of crabs:

My grandchildren left a stone on the porch with a crab planted on top of it. Normally I would have cringed. I didn't realize I had a problem with crabs until it was noticeable that it had gone. The strange thing is, my grandchildren have not since tried to terrorize me with the mice. It is as if I manifested their torments by my own fear.

Fear of Policemen

Hannah was a middle-aged woman who had grown up terrified of policemen. She had no idea where this fear had stemmed from but had tried suggestion hypnosis and, although it had helped in other aspects of her life, she was still left with this fear. When she was regressed, her subconscious quickly came up with the answers.

She was aged approximately 5 years old and was being naughty one evening. She had been sent straight to bed without her supper. Her father told her that the police were on their way to arrest her and take her to prison.

As she was feeling very frightened, she heard heavy footsteps on the stairs. This terrified her and she lay in her bed trembling with anticipation, expecting to be punished. She was horrified at the thought of having to go to prison. Her little life was crumbling.

Hannah found it easy to laugh at the incident now she was an adult. She was able to recall the footsteps, now the memory had been brought back to her conscious through hypnosis. Her father's attempts to frighten her were very successful but, unfortunately, more hideous and long-lasting than he could have anticipated.

Fear of Knives

As long as Tina could remember she had been terrified of knives. She felt like some kind of freak, unable as she was to handle any kind of knife. Her problem was so severe that she had to have someone else cut up her food for her. Even then she could only eat her food with a fork and spoon. Just the thought of a knife lying about would make her break out into a cold sweat. She felt she had become a social outcast.

She would visualize someone picking up a knife and slitting their own throat. Even the thought of a knife brought this terror. When she was regressed, she was a little girl watching a film about Jack the Ripper. It was such a shock to see someone's throat being slit that she had fused the fear with the knife. The fear manifested another reaction: Every time she saw or thought of a knife she experienced that terror and became even more frightened of the fear – a terrible circle of negative and destructive thoughts. There are many examples of TV programmes or films affecting the young. A diet of violent videos can create trance, and viewing excess violence can desensitize a young, vulnerable mind to the subject, creating a lack of compassion in the person as he or she grows to maturity. This has not been proved by statistics but I have certainly come across this many times in therapy. It really is a case of common sense: If you can get used to watching operations and became a surgeon, it stands to reason you could get so used to violence that it no longer has any meaning for you.

Weight Anxiety

Susan was a 17-year-old bulimic. She would regularly overeat and then make herself throw it all back up.

When regressed, Susan went to a time when she was very young. She had been ill and watching TV in bed. There had been a TV documentary film depicting the life of a teenager who had anorexia, showing the horrors of the girl's existence.

She eventually died. It was based on truth and had created, in Susan, being as she was in a depressed state from her illness, a certain vulnerability. In her subconscious she had created a survival technique to prevent her from dying of a food disorder. She over-compensated by eating plenty and then, so as not to put on weight, she made herself sick. An example of a 'corrupted mind file' created from a traumatic incident when vulnerable.

As a result of our regression work, Susan came to recognize the origins of her fear both of death and of overweight.

Fear of Worms

Jane had an irrational fear of worms. The man she loved was a keen weekend fisherman and he wanted her to share his hobby. Her absolute terror of worms prevented her from doing this and was affecting their relationship.

When she was regressed she spoke in the whimpering tones of a small child. 'I'm in the garden with my sister,' she reported. 'No, don't do it PLEASE! I'm afraid!' She explained that her sister was going to put the worms in her hand. She started to scream: 'No! No! Don't! … Oh no!' She was reliving the experience. Her sister made her grasp the worms and then held Jane's hand so tightly that it made her squeeze the worms. This experience created a trauma-related horror that was deeply buried.

After the therapy Jane was later able happily to join her boyfriend on his fishing expeditions. They married and both became happy weekend fishermen.

Low Self-esteem

Memories can go right back to being born and the birth itself. Some people relive the memory of their own birth in every detail, recalling experiences such as breech deliveries and the tightening of the umbilical cord around their neck.

One man I regressed had such a low self-esteem that he was apologetic even for being alive in the first place. When he was regressed, he had just been born and the midwife had remarked as she saw him: 'He's too weak even to breathe!' Even though a baby doesn't know the language, it is still recorded and can become available to a new set of programmes generated by other negative incidents.

Fear of Blushing All Over

In my profession and research I have encountered some very unusual phobias. One of the most interesting was of a young man whom I will call Guy. He was a male stripper who came to see a colleague of mine.

Guy said he had just become aware of a phobia that was interfering with his very lucrative profession. He had a very good act stripping for ladies' hen nights in pubs and clubs around England. However, he had suddenly started to blush when he took his clothes off, and this was spoiling his routine. He said he felt very confident on stage, but the blushing suggested quite the opposite! What was going on in his inner mind to sabotage his profession? His inner mind seemed to have a mind of its own!

Fear of Buttons

When two people have a phobia about the same object, it is always surprising to see how completely unrelated the underlying causes can be. To give you an example, I will highlight two clients, one male and one female.

Henry reported that he couldn't bear to see buttons. He would break out into a sweat at the mere sight of them. When regressed he went to a time when he was a little boy of about four. He was experiencing himself being dressed up in little girls' dresses by his grandmother. She was fondling him sexually and, although he it wasn't unpleasant, he knew that it 'just didn't feel right'. He did not consciously remember this incident, although after hypnosis he could recall it.

Since the therapy, other memories came forward, resembling a jigsaw puzzle. As the pieces come together, Henry's behaviour started to make sense. He was able to come to terms with what had happened to him, and combat his fear successfully.

Betty also had a fear of buttons and suffered similar unfortunate stress effects at the sight of them. In her case there had been no sexual abuse but she had always been criticized severely as a child, resulting in her having very little sense of self-worth. Painfully shy and introverted, she had linked the buttons to eyes watching her. One of her dolls may have had buttons for eyes, which had perhaps triggered the frustration and hatred she felt surrounding those loved ones who had mistreated her.

Again, in a short space of time Betty was able to recognize and overcome her fear.

Fear of Injections

Mario was a famous interior designer who had a serious fear of injections. He was so frightened that he would be quite ill for two weeks before he had to have any injection. He needed to travel and this phobia was restricting his business abroad. When he came to see me he reported that he had always been afraid of injections and asked me whether I thought it was possible that his mother may have had an injection when he was in the womb, which was now affecting him. He just couldn't understand where this fear had originated from. I honestly didn't know if it could have started in the womb. I hadn't personally had experience at this time of someone going so far back in regression, but I kept an open mind.

When I regressed Mario to the first time he had an injection he was aged three or four. He remembered being in the corridor of what looked like an old school. He was led into a room where some children were being injected. He experienced himself calmly sitting on a bed while the doctor injected him. He was happily chewing some sweets the doctor had given him. He was quite comfortable with this. I asked how he felt; he shrugged his shoulders and said 'OK!' – he wasn't experiencing any discomfort at all. But after the injection he started to frown and said his mother was agitated and had started to hug him. The doctor, too, looked anxious and afraid, and this shocked Mario into thinking that perhaps he was behaving incorrectly – perhaps he should also be worried.

His mind then over-compensated and the next time he had to have an injection he caused a terrible fuss. He repeated this throughout his life; whenever he had to have an injection he became agitated, aggressive and scared.

When Mario came out of hypnosis he was stunned. He now realized that he hadn't always had a fear of injections and that he had literally been taught to be frightened. 'His' fear had actually been brought on by his mother's distress, which had got confused in his mind with the experience of the injection itself.

'We are what we pretend to be.' I remember one episode in my own life that offers another example of this: I was staying in a lovely manor house with a swimming pool and wonderful facilities. One of the residents was a rather arrogant pop singer. He was very flirtatious and in order to put him off I pretended to swoon over him, knowing this behaviour was usually a turn-off. It started as a joke, but the joke ended up on me. A few days later, I forgot I was pretending and experienced a type of over-reaction. I'd actually started to believe I had a crush on this obnoxious character. I was lovesick. My mind had been fooled.

Many people go through their lives with this type of mistaken 'programming', which can be so easily rectified.

Fear of His Own Penis

Terry was an alcoholic who led a very isolated and lonely life. He was in his sixties and had never had sex. When he was regressed it took him to a time when he was about 4. He was in the bath and was, out of curiosity as toddlers and very young children do, playing with his penis. His mother saw him and went hysterical, calling him dirty and smacking him until he screamed. Still in regression, Terry moved to an incident a few months later, at the doctor's surgery. His mother must have discussed the bath-time incident with the doctor, and they'd decided to try to frighten him out of playing with himself again. The doctor held a large knife above Terry's penis and said that if Terry touched himself again he would have to cut his penis off. He made Terry promise faithfully that he wouldn't touch his penis again for anything but necessity. His mother had no idea of the damage she was inflicting and neither did the doctor. Fortunately, these days most of us are aware of what we say in front of children. They can be so vulnerable and when shocked the trauma can lead to a lifetime's worth of destructive or harmful (to themselves or others) behaviour.

With hypnotherapy Terry was able to understand the source of his phobia and live a happier life.

Fear of Toilets

Ray, an executive, had a fear of public toilets. He just couldn't bring himself to use them. He had only noticed his acute reaction the previous year. When I regressed him he was travelling in his car on the motorway, listening to his favourite radio talk show. The subject being discussed was phobias and he was curiously listening to a man saying how he was afraid of going into public toilets since he had been attacked in one when he was small. That was it – Ray had somehow latched on to the fear himself!

This fear was easily cleared with suggestion therapy.

Fear of Fish

Jeremy had a severe fear of fish. If he was swimming he had a horror of fish passing him, how they would feel and where they were if he didn't see any.

This problem was cleared using the television screen method mentioned earlier (*page 72*). Jeremy visualized himself feeding the fish out of his hand. After the therapy he became a diver. He recently sent me a postcard while on holiday, expressing his pride in his new hobby.

Telephone Hang-up

This could be called 'the case of the man with 101 phobias.' Originally he came for help with overcoming his fear of telephones. He couldn't pick one up. If he was forced to, he would stutter and forget what to say. He would literally go to pieces. If he was at home, his wife always answered the phone or he would just let it ring. He had recently started at a new job, which he enjoyed, but he could not avoid hiding his fear any longer. Jobs were too hard to come by, so he decided to try and cure his fear.

When he was regressed, it appeared that when he'd been young every time the phone went there always seemed to be bad news. His mother would answer it and be in a bad mood and, many times, cry. His father was in the air force and quite a tyrant. They were constantly moving to different camps, never settling in one place for long. Once when he was tiny he answered the phone himself and it was his uncle, who was an alcoholic and very drunk at the time. He frightened little Sam so much it made him cry. Another time there was a death and then an accident in the family within a matter of weeks, which they were told of by phone. In short, Sam's family often found themselves in a state of turmoil.

As sessions continued, I discovered that Sam also had a fear of eating. He was terrified of becoming fat like Billy Bunter. He would stop eating altogether and then binge. If he had even a tiny meal he would tell himself he felt full. This would trigger an uncontrollable feeling to eat. He was afraid of junk food because that was what Billy Bunter ate, but stuffed himself with it anyway. This resulted in incredible feelings of remorse, guilt and loneliness, synonymous with the phobic and the person with a severe eating disorder.

The telephone phobia was cleared and Sam is now in line for promotion. He is also more in control of the other phobias he suffers from.

Fear of Spiders

Katy, a very shy woman, had a terror of spiders but could not understand where it had come from because she wasn't frightened by any other insects – in fact she liked them. In regression she was taken to when she went to a friend's house after school as a young girl. She wasn't supposed to have been there, as she was meant to have gone straight home that day. Her friend's house was empty and they were playing in a bedroom. It was up a flight of stairs which were quite dark. As they were playing, her friend's mother came home. They didn't want to get caught in the rooms that were out of bounds, and so they had to both rush downstairs. As Katy started to run down she saw a big spider. She wasn't scared, it just surprised her. She did what she could to avoid treading on it and in so doing she fell down the stairs, breaking her leg. This had been where her fear had started. It was a fear of injury but had manifested in the fear of spiders, since the spider was the reminder of her pain, guilt and fear.

Suggestion hypnosis alone may not have been enough to free Katy from this fear, but as she herself wanted to know its deeper cause, we used regression to achieve the same end.

Hates Men but Loves Cake

Louise was very overweight and could not stop eating chocolate. She also had a phobia about men. She couldn't bear them to touch her. She disliked them intensely and it had affected her all through her life.

When regressed she went to a time when she was a little girl and wore her hair in plaits. She was in her bedroom playing and had got hold of a pair of scissors. She started to experiment by cutting off one of her plaits. Her mother came in just as she was about to cut off the other but, of course, it was too late – she had ruined her lovely hair and her mother went mad, shouting and screaming. When Louise started to cry, her mother apologized and gave her a big wedge of chocolate cake to settle her down. Six months later she was playing in the classroom and swinging between two desks when she fell. She caught her eye on the desk and a splinter pierced her eye. She was in hysterics and once again she was given chocolate, but this time it was an entire cake. When she'd calmed down a bit she was taken to hospital to have the splinter removed. She was so frightened that it took three male nurses to hold her down. The whole thing got fused together: she hated the restriction of being held down by men and made a mental vow never to let men hold her down again. Although she was only a little girl, this instruction stayed with her all her life and manifested itself in many ways. She associated men with fear and pain, chocolate with comfort.

In hypnosis through these associations, she came to see for herself how her child-self had misconstrued both the source of her pain and that of her comfort.

Panic Attacks with Wasps

Jenny was frightened of wasps. She was so scared, the mere thought of them gave her a panic attack. But it wasn't a fear of wasps that had caused her attacks in the first place.

When was regressed she was in a garden looking at some beautiful flowers. Her grandmother saw a wasp and ran over to her, screaming and flapping her arms about. She pulled Jenny aside and gave her a long lecture about the dangers of wasps. Since then the thought of wasps brought on the fear and panic she experienced when she was a child.

After uncovering the underlying cause of her panic attacks, simple suggestion therapy was able to help Jenny combat them.

Cupboard Anxiety

Joan had a fear of cupboards. When she was regressed she went back to when she was 3. An uncle had locked her in a cupboard under the stairs. It was pitch black and only a tiny space. There was a mouse in the cupboard; she didn't know what it was but could feel it running over her feet.

Once this reason was uncovered and dealt with I was able to help Joan to reprogramme her responses.

❖ ❖ ❖

CHOOSING YOUR THERAPIST

A Suggestion hypnotherapy should not normally be too expensive. However, if you use a top specialist in the field, then the price will reflect this. This is the case in any profession, but the advantage is it may only take a few sessions to be cured of your problem.

You can work with self-hypnosis to clear your phobia, but if you find after a few months that you have made no progress, or if you still have not accomplished your positive goals, it may be helpful to consult a professional. Sometimes someone who is trained to recognize and guide in hypnosis or hypnotherapy will make all the difference.

You can accomplish your goals by working on your own, but certain problems or circumstances lend themselves better to treatment by a professional.

You might wonder how to find the correct therapist with the appropriate training. Choosing the right professional is an individual matter. There are a great many available, but you need to ask if they are trained in regression therapy and how long they believe it will take to clear the problem, also what success rate do they believe that they can accomplish.

Another consideration is the approach taken by the professional you choose. For more information, consult the Useful Addresses chapter.

FURTHER READING
AND USEFUL ADDRESSES

Banish Anxiety by Dr Kenneth Hambley (Thorsons)

For Ever Young by Marisa Peer (Michael Joseph)

Guide to Stress Reduction by L. John Mason, PhD (Glendale, CA: Westwood Publishing)

Mind Machines You Can Build by G. Harry Stine (Florida: Top of the Mountain Publishing)

The Self Healing Personality by Howard S. Friedman (New York: Henry Holt & Co)

Self-hypnosis by Valerie Austin (Thorsons)

Slim While You Sleep by Valerie Austin (London: Blake Publishing)

Think and Grow Rich by Napoleon Hill (Thorsons)

USEFUL ADDRESSES

For private therapy, training courses and information on cassette tapes and books:

The Austin Training Centre
Chesham House
5th Floor
150 Regent Street
London W1R 5FA
Tel. 0181–569 7192
Fax 0181–560 0815

The Austin Institute of Structural Hypnosis
20/24 Cerok Linchai, 07000 Kedawang
Langkawi Kedah Darul Aman
Malaysia
Tel. 04 955 2586
Fax. 04 955 2633

For full update information and brochure on-line:
http://www.paradiselearning.com

For information on the International Register of
Hypnotherapy and hypnotherapists in the UK, contact:
Gil Boyne
American Council of Hypnotherapist Examiners
1147 East Broadway
Suite 340, Glendale
CA 91205
Tel. 818 247 9379

In other countries:

Margaret Tomko
PO Box 197
Sylvania, Southgate
NSW 2224
Australia
Tel. 02 522 8306

Arone Eldan
RR 1 Site 5 Box 91
St Albert
Alberta T8N 1M8
Canada
Tel. 403 460 2442

James Marsh
5 Kooba Street
Box 948, Griffith
NSW 2680
Australia
Tel. 069 624 264

Dr Patrick Yeung
PO Box 73589
Kowloon Central PO
Kowloon
Hong Kong
Tel. 852 2782 7415

Kelvyn Johnston
13 Belmont Lane
Musselburgh
Dunnedin
New Zealand
Tel. 03 455 4452

Vernon Frost
12 Liddesdale Road
Pinelands
Cape Town 7405
South Africa
Tel. 021 531 3436

INDEX